GUIDE TO THE
FLIGHT
REVIEW

For Pilots & Instructors

JACKIE SPANITZ

SEVENTH EDITION

COMPLETE PREPARATION FOR ISSUING OR
TAKING A FLIGHT REVIEW INCLUDING BOTH
THE GROUND AND FLIGHT REQUIREMENTS

with excerpts from Michael Hayes'
popular *Oral Exam Guide* series

Aviation Supplies & Academics, Inc.
Newcastle, Washington

Guide to the Flight Review for Pilots & Instructors
Seventh Edition
by Jackie Spanitz

Aviation Supplies & Academics, Inc.
7005 132nd Place SE
Newcastle, Washington 98059-3153

Go to **www.asa2fly.com/reader/oegbfr** for further resources associated with
this book. Also, visit the ASA website often (**www.asa2fly.com**, Product
Updates link or search "OEG-BFR") to find updates posted there due to FAA
regulation revisions that may affect this book.

Portions of this book were previously published in the *Private Oral Exam
Guide* by Michael D. Hayes.

ASA-OEG-BFR7
ISBN 978-1-61954-082-8

Printed in the United States of America
2016   2015   2014   2013   9 8 7 6 5 4 3 2 1

Library of Congress Cataloging-in-Publication Data
Spanitz, Jackie
   Guide to the Biennial Flight Review: complete preparation for
   issuing or taking a Flight Review; with excerpts from Michael
   Hayes' popular oral exam guide series / by Jackie Spanitz.
        p.   cm.
   1. Airplanes—Piloting. 2. United States. Federal Aviation
   Administration—Examinations.   I.Title
   TL710.5622   1994
   629.132'52'076—dc20   94-36559
                                                    CIP

Contents

4 Flight Instruction Requirement

Introduction

1 Introduction

What is the Flight Review?

This guide to the flight review (previously called "Biennial Flight Review" or BFR) is a comprehensive guide to prepare for taking or issuing a flight review. The flight review has been an FAA requirement since 1974 and was developed to curb pilot-related accidents. Although it has accomplished this objective, there is still room for improvement. A standard flight review should offer an effective learning experience that will further reduce pilot-related accidents. The FAA's guidance document reprinted in Appendix 3 provides some excellent and very specific recommendations on how to use the flight review in this capacity.

There has been confusion about the nature of the flight review. It is not intended to be another checkride, but rather an assessment of the pilot's skills, with the sole objective to determine if the pilot is safe in the operations he/she usually conducts. With this in mind, this guide will prepare and offer some guidance to those taking or issuing a flight review.

Again, the flight review is meant to determine your ability to handle the airplane safely and with good judgment. It is not meant to be like the checkride, but rather instructional. The maneuvers performed in the flight should reflect the pilot's experience and type of flying; the actions should be predictable to the instructor and conform to local procedures, with safety being the main concern. The flight review should be considered an opportunity. It could be performed annually, as recurrent or refresher training, or biennially, as required by 14 CFR §61.56.

Flight Review Candidates

14 CFR §61.56 states that every pilot must take a flight review every 24 calendar months. This means *every* pilot must take a flight review in order to maintain pilot-in-command (PIC) privileges.

Requirements (14 CFR 61.56)

The conduct of the flight review is at the discretion of the flight instructor, but the FAA does state minimum requirements necessary for the satisfactory completion:

- 1 hour of flight training and 1 hour of ground training
- A review of 14 CFR Part 91
- A review of those maneuvers and procedures necessary for the pilot to demonstrate the safe exercise of the privileges of the pilot certificate
- A logbook endorsement stating the satisfactory completion of the check

See Appendix 1 for the complete 14 CFR §61.56, and Appendix 3 for the FAA's recommendations on content and best use of time during the flight review.

Options for Completing the Flight Review

With safety in mind, the flight review can be completed in a manner beneficial to the pilot:

- *A flight review with a flight instructor*

Everyone can use some dual flight periodically. This would be a prime opportunity to brush up on skills not frequently used. If flights normally take place at a nontowered airport, flight into a busier airport could increase proficiency in radio communications, and airspace. If straight and level is the normal attitude, some unusual attitudes and hood-work would be beneficial. If flights are normally conducted within the local area, a cross-country could be planned.

This is the suggested route to take for those that don't have the opportunity to fly as frequently as they might like—work off that rust! *See* Appendix 3 for the FAA's recommendations on how to conduct an effective flight review.

• *Upgrade your pilot certificate*

The FAA does not specify which aircraft a candidate must use for the flight review (however, this might change in the future). With this in mind, this would be a prime opportunity to get that instrument rating, sea rating, multi-engine rating, glider license, or helicopter license. Any checkride meets the requirements of a flight review, so the sky's the limit! The FAA also states the flight review requirements can be accomplished in combination with other recency requirements: interpreted, this means candidates can become night current, instrument current, or tailwheel current (keep in mind that additional tasks will be added to meet both requirements).

This is the suggested route for those who are flying frequently, have little rust on their skills, and who are looking to expand their flying horizons. Again, safety is the main issue, and careful consideration should be taken before deciding which aircraft will be used. The NTSB suggests taking the flight review in the aircraft most frequently flown, or the most complicated aircraft for which you are rated.

• *The **WINGS** Program*

A person who has satisfactorily completed one or more phases of an FAA-sponsored pilot proficiency award program (the **WINGS** Program) meets the requirements of a flight review. This program was developed as a way to promote proficiency and safety, while providing a motivation for pilots to do so. What pilot doesn't feel satisfaction with an earned pair of wings?

It's a great program that gives pilots the opportunity to attend FAA safety seminars, participate in online courses—and be rewarded for meeting the regulatory requirements. See Appendix 4 and visit **www.faasafety.gov** for more information on the **WINGS** Program.

Conduct of the Flight Review

Although the regulation (14 CFR 61.56, *see* Appendix 1) does not specify which maneuvers should be included in a flight review, the FAA has provided some guidance to include suggested procedures. Ultimately the contents of a flight review are at the discretion of the flight instructor, but for a consistent and thorough check, consult AC 61-98B (*see* Appendix 2), and the FAA's Guidance Document: "Conducting an Effective Flight Review" (*see* Appendix 3).

The flight review should be conducted in an efficient manner, meeting the 1 hour ground and 1 hour flight requirement, without being excessive.

The following FAA documents are used as references throughout the book. Be sure to use the latest revision of each document when preparing for your flight review:

14 CFR Part 43	*Maintenance, preventive maintenance, rebuilding, and alteration*
14 CFR Part 61	*Certification: Pilots, flight instructors, and ground instructors*
14 CFR Part 91	*General operating and flight rules*
NTSB Part 830	*Notification and reporting of aircraft accidents and incidents*
AC 00-6A	*Aviation Weather*
AC 00-45	*Aviation Weather Services*
AC 60-22	*Aeronautical Decision Making*
FAA-H-8083-3	*Airplane Flying Handbook*
FAA-H-8083-15	*Instrument Flying Handbook*
FAA-H-8083-25	*Pilot's Handbook of Aeronautical Knowledge*
AIM	*Aeronautical Information Manual*

Reader Resources

See also the Reader Resource page on the ASA website at **www.asa2fly.com/reader/oegbfr** for more related materials to supplement or update the information in this book.

Q&A:
Questions Most Commonly
Asked About the Flight Review
2

Candidate Information

1. Who must take the flight review?

All pilots who wish to exercise their pilot-in-command (PIC) privilege and do not meet the exemptions listed below. A pilot would be in violation of 14 CFR §61.56 if he/she acts as pilot-in-command after the expiration date of the flight review.

2. What procedures would exempt a pilot from the flight review requirement?

The following serve as exemptions from the flight review:

14 CFR §61.58 pilot proficiency check
14 CFR Part 121 pilot proficiency check
14 CFR Part 135 pilot proficiency check
14 CFR Part 141 chief pilot proficiency check
Military pilot proficiency check
Any proficiency check administered by the FAA
Pilot examiner annual flight check
Checkride for any certificate or rating
Procedures specifically authorized by the FAA
Satisfactory completion of any phase of the FAA *WINGS* program

3. Who can issue a flight review?

Any current flight instructor or other person designated by the FAA.

4. Is the FAA notified of an unsuccessful flight review?

No. The logbook endorsement states only satisfactory completion of the flight review. If the person issuing the flight review does not give the pilot the required endorsement, that pilot has the option of getting some dual instruction in the inadequate areas, or taking the flight review with another flight instructor.

5. Can an instrument proficiency check (IPC) serve as a flight review?

No. By itself, the instrument proficiency check serves only that purpose; however, the two functions can be combined in the same flight. This calls for meeting both requirements and 2 separate endorsements for the proficiency check and the flight review.

6. Do student pilots require a flight review?

No. Flight reviews are required only by pilots holding a sport, recreational, private, commercial, flight instructor, or airline transport pilot certificate.

7. Why are flight reviews required?

The purpose of the flight review is to assess a pilot's skills in performing a *safe* flight.

8. A pilot's last flight review was completed on 3-22-13. When will it expire?

Flight reviews are current for 24 calendar months. This flight review would expire 3-31-15, or the last day of the month.

9. If a pilot has not had a flight review for more than 2 years, is his/her pilot certificate invalid?

No. Pilot certificates are issued for life, or until surrendered, suspended or revoked. Without a current flight review, however, the pilot may not act as PIC of an aircraft.

10. Can a pilot fly solo (be the sole occupant of the airplane) without a current flight review?

No. Solo flight requires the pilot to act as PIC which is illegal without a current flight review.

11. Does a pilot have to possess a current medical certificate to satisfactorily complete a flight review?

No. But the pilot may not act as PIC, either during the flight review or any time thereafter, until medical eligibility has been obtained. This is a driver's license for sport pilot privileges, or a third-class medical certificate for private pilots.

12. What do recreational/private pilots and higher need in order to fly light-sport aircraft (LSA)?

Your existing pilot's license is also your sport pilot certificate—no new certification is needed. If your medical has expired, you can use your driver's license as your medical eligibility to fly LSA. However, if your medical has been denied or revoked, you must clear it to use your driver's license as your medical in the future.

13. If a flight review is rendered unsatisfactory, does the pilot have to return to the same flight instructor for another attempt?

No. The pilot has the choice of using any authorized instructor.

14. Without a current flight review, may an instructor endorse a pilot's logbook for solo flight to prepare for the flight review?

No. Solo flight requires the pilot to act as PIC which is illegal without a current flight review. This would not be necessary anyway, because the flight review is not a test, but rather an instructional flight assessing the pilot's skills in performing a safe flight.

15. If a pilot is presently taking dual lessons, do they have to take a flight review?

Yes. Dual lessons can only qualify as a flight review if the flight instructor conducts the lesson with those intentions, meets the requirements specified in 14 CFR §61.56, and issues the endorsement after a satisfactory completion of the flight.

16. Can a pilot ask a flight instructor for a flight review endorsement without actually flying the review?

No. As required by 14 CFR §61.56, 1 hour of flight and 1 hour of ground training is required to qualify as a flight review.

17. Does a pilot have to get a flight review in each category and class of aircraft for which they are rated?

No. The satisfactory completion of the flight review allows pilots to exercise PIC privileges in all categories and classes of aircraft for which they are rated. However, since safety is the main issue, pilots may elect to get a flight review in each category and class held on their pilot certificates.

18. Does the flight review have to include all the maneuvers contained in the Practical Test Standards?

No. The pilot is required to perform only those maneuvers and procedures determined by the flight instructor as necessary to demonstrate the safe exercise of the privileges of the pilot certificate. However, this implies that the pilot should be able to perform at the level recognized by each certificate. *See* Pages 4-3 and 4-4.

19. Is there a written examination required by the FAA for completion of a flight review?

No. There is not a requirement for a written; however, the candidate must demonstrate knowledge of the general operating and flight rules of Part 91, and the flight instructor may choose to do this through a written or oral exercise. Many flight instructors ask candidates to complete a short written review before meeting to complete the flight review. *See* Page 3-63.

Another option is for the applicant to complete the FAA's online course for the flight review. This scenario-based multiple-choice quiz reviews Part 91 and the AIM in preparation for your next flight review. Upon successful completion of the course you can print a certificate of achievement. This course is available at **www.faasafety.gov**; select the Learning Center tab, and follow the links for the available Online Courses.

20. How can a pilot prove satisfactory completion of a flight review?

The satisfactory completion of a flight review requires a logbook endorsement by the flight instructor giving the review.

This endorsement may appear as follows:

I certify that (First name, MI, Last name), (pilot certificate), (certificate number), has satisfactorily completed a flight review of §61.56(a) on (date).

S/S   [date]   J.J. Jones   987654321 CFI   Exp. 01-31-14

21. Does the logbook endorsement mean the pilot must carry his/her logbook at all times as proof of the completion of the flight review?

No. The pilot must present the endorsement only when asked by an authority (FAA, NTSB, law enforcement officer, etc.), or by a Fixed Base Operator (FBO) in order to rent an aircraft.

Note: Sport pilots must carry with them a logbook endorsement (a copy or separate card is sometimes used so the pilot does not have to carry the complete logbook) of their category/class of aircraft, but not the flight review.

22. How should the flight review be logged?

If the pilot is the sole manipulator of the controls, then the flight should be logged as PIC time. If receiving dual instruction, then it should be logged as dual. The pilot-in-command should be determined between the candidate and the flight instructor before beginning the review flight.

23. Must the aircraft being used be IFR equipped?

The airplane must have the instruments required for the type of flight operations you intend to conduct. This should be discussed between the flight instructor and candidate during the preflight phase of the review.

24. Must the aircraft have dual controls?

No. However if the airplane does not have dual controls, the pilot must be qualified to act as PIC with medical eligibility and be current (within the 24 month flight review window).

25. Can a ground trainer be used exclusively for the flight review?

Yes. A flight simulator or flight training device may be used as long as it meets the following requirements: the ground trainer must be used in accordance with an approved course under 14 CFR Part 142; it must be approved for landings; and it must represent an aircraft for which the pilot is rated.

Instructor Information

26. Who acts as PIC during the flight review?

PIC should be determined prior to the flight so there is a clear understanding of responsibilities. This decision should be made after inspecting the pilot's logbook, pilot certificate, and medical certificate to ensure the candidate is qualified to act as PIC.

27. What is the minimum time required for a satisfactory flight review?

14 CFR §61.56 requires 1 hour of flight and 1 hour of ground training.

28. What subjects should be covered during the ground training?

The FAA specifies only a knowledge of 14 CFR Part 91. The objective of the flight review is safe flight by the candidate, so each ground training should be tailored to the pilot's experience, and type of flight normally conducted. This is a learning experience— the training should be broad enough to be comprehensive, yet have enough depth to provide a forum for learning.

Encourage your students to complete the FAA's online course for the flight review before meeting, to lay the groundwork for your ground training. This scenario-based multiple-choice quiz reviews Part 91 and the AIM in preparation for your next flight review. Upon successful completion of the course you can print a certificate of achievement. This course is available at

www.faasafety.gov; select the Learning Center tab, and follow the links for the available Online Courses.

29. What maneuvers are required during the flight portion of the flight review?

The FAA specifies only those maneuvers and procedures which, at the discretion of the person giving the review, are necessary for the pilot to demonstrate the safe exercise of the privileges of the pilot certificate. AC 61-98B (*see* Appendix 2), and the Flight Review Checklist (*see* Appendix 5) provide more specific advice as to the conduct of the flight review.

30. Which ratings are required for a flight instructor to conduct flight reviews?

The aircraft category and class used for the flight review must appear on the flight instructor's certificate.

31. Must the flight instructor possess a current medical certificate to conduct a flight review?

No. However, this would force the role of PIC on to the candidate; it should be determined in the preflight phase of the review if he/she is qualified for this responsibility.

32. Is the flight instructor required to have five hours of PIC flight time in each make and model of aircraft in which the flight review is going to be conducted?

If using a general aviation aircraft, no: the instructor must only be rated in the aircraft. However, if using a light-sport aircraft (LSA), the instructor must have at least 5 hours of flight time in a make and model within the same set of aircraft.

33. What responsibilities does the flight instructor have following a flight review?

Upon completion of a flight review, the flight instructor should debrief the pilot and inform him/her whether the review was satisfactory or unsatisfactory. Either way, the candidate should be provided with a comprehensive analysis of his/her performance, including any weak areas. If the flight review was satisfactory, the candidate's logbook must be endorsed accordingly. If the review is unsatisfactory, no logbook endorsement should be made.

34. How should the flight time be logged by the flight instructor?

The flight instructor should log the flight review as PIC time, as per 14 CFR §61.51(e)(3).

35. Is the instructor required to keep a record of all flight reviews administered?

No, it is not required; however, it is highly recommended that they do so.

36. Are flight instructors required to get flight reviews?

Yes. Unless they meet the exemptions listed in question 2, all pilots are required to meet the flight review requirement.

37. Can a flight instructor endorse his/her own logbook for the satisfactory completion of a flight review?

No. According to 14 CFR §61.195(i) and §61.421, flight instructors shall not make any self-endorsement for a certificate, rating, flight review, authorization, operating privilege, practical test, or knowledge test.

38. Do flight instructors have to go to the FAA for a flight review?

No. Any authorized flight instructor may conduct the flight review.

39. Do flight instructor refresher courses (FIRC) serve as a flight review?

No. Refresher courses do not meet all of the flight review requirements; however, they do meet the one hour ground training requirement.

Ground Instruction Requirement

3

3 Ground Instruction Requirement

There is a 1 hour requirement for ground training dictated by 14 CFR §61.56 that involves the review of the current general operating and flight rules of 14 CFR Part 91. This can be accomplished in one of three ways: through an oral exercise, a written exercise, or a combination of both. The FAA's online Flight Review course (available at **www.faasafety.gov**) is an excellent way to meet the ground training requirement.

Review: Sample Oral Exercise

A. Privileges and Limitations

1. **To act as pilot-in-command or in any other capacity as a required flight crewmember of a civil aircraft, what must a pilot have in his/her physical possession or readily accessible in the aircraft?** (14 CFR 61.3)

   a. A pilot certificate (or special purpose pilot authorization).

   b. An appropriate current medical certificate (except for balloon, glider, and LSA operations).

   c. A photo ID (such as a driver's license, government ID card, military ID card, or passport).

2. **What privileges and limitations apply to a recreational/ private pilot using a driver's license as medical eligibility to exercise sport pilot privileges to operate a light-sport aircraft?** (14 CFR 61.315)

   Recreational/private pilots and above can fly LSA with no additional tests or endorsements. However, a number of limitations apply when using the driver's license as medical eligibility, including:

   a. You can share the operating expenses of a flight with a passenger, provided the expenses involve only fuel, oil, airport expenses, or aircraft rental fees. You must pay at least half the operating expenses of the flight.

   Continued

b. You *cannot* act as pilot-in-command of an LSA:

- that is carrying a passenger or property for compensation or hire.
- for compensation or hire.
- in furtherance of a business.
- while carrying more than one passenger.
- at night.
- in Class A airspace.
- outside the U.S., unless you have prior authorization from the country in which you seek to operate. (Your sport pilot certificate carries the limit "Holder does not meet ICAO requirements.")
- to demonstrate the aircraft in flight to a prospective buyer if you are an aircraft salesperson.
- in a passenger-carrying airlift sponsored by a charitable organization.
- at an altitude of more than 10,000 feet MSL.
- when the flight or surface visibility is less than 3 statute miles.
- without visual reference to the surface.
- contrary to any operating limitation placed on the airworthiness certificate of the aircraft being flown.
- contrary to any limit or endorsement on your pilot certificate, airman medical certificate, or any other limit or endorsement from an authorized instructor.
- contrary to any restriction or limitation on your U.S. driver's license or any restriction or limitation imposed by judicial or administrative order when using your driver's license to satisfy a requirement of this part.
- while towing any object.
- as a pilot flight crewmember on any aircraft for which more than one pilot is required by the type certificate of the aircraft or the regulations under which the flight is conducted.

B. Currency Requirements

1. What are the requirements to remain current as a private pilot? (14 CFR 61.56, 61.57)

a. Accomplish a flight review given in an aircraft for which that pilot is rated by an authorized instructor within the preceding 24 calendar months.

b. To carry passengers, a pilot must have made within the preceding 90 days:
- Three takeoffs and three landings as the sole manipulator of the flight controls of an aircraft of the same category and class and, if a type rating is required, of the same type.
- If the aircraft is a tailwheel airplane, the landings must have been made to a full stop.
- If operations are to be conducted during the period beginning 1 hour after sunset to 1 hour before sunrise, with passengers on board, the pilot-in-command must have, within the preceding 90 days, made at least three takeoffs and three landings to a full stop during that period in an aircraft of the same category, class, and type (if a type rating is required) of aircraft to be used.

2. What are the various types and durations of medical certificates required? (14 CFR 61.23)

Student pilot, recreational pilot, and private pilot operations, other than glider and balloon pilots require a Third-Class Medical Certificate, which expires at the end of:

1. The 60th month after the month of the date of the examination shown on the certificate if the person has not reached his or her 40th birthday on or before the date of examination; or

2. The 24th month after the month of the date of examination shown on the certificate if the person has reached his or her 40th birthday on or before the date of the examination.

The holder of a Second-Class Medical Certificate may exercise commercial privileges during the first 12 calendar months, but the certificate is valid only for private pilot privileges during the following (12 or 48) calendar months, depending on the applicant's age.

Continued

The holder of a First-Class Medical Certificate may exercise Airline Transport Pilot privileges during the first 12 calendar months, commercial privileges during the following 6 calendar months, and private pilot privileges during the following (12 or 48) calendar months, depending on the applicant's age.

In other words, a medical certificate may last 6 months to a year with first-class privileges, 12 months (from the date of the examination) with second-class privileges, and 2 or 5 years with third-class privileges, depending on whether the applicant is above or below 40 years of age.

C. Aircraft Certificates and Documents

1. What documents are required on board an aircraft prior to flight? (14 CFR 91.203, 91.9)

A irworthiness certificate
R egistration certificate
O wner's manual or operating limitations
W eight and balance data

2. Does an aircraft's registration certificate have an expiration date? (14 CFR 47.40)

Yes; As of October 1, 2010, specific registration expiration dates have been established for all aircraft registered before October 1, 2010. Those aircraft require re-registration according to a specific schedule. All initial aircraft registrations issued on or after October 1, 2010, will expire three years after the last day of the month in which they were issued.

D. Aircraft Maintenance Requirements

1. Who is responsible for ensuring that an aircraft is maintained in an airworthy condition? (14 CFR 91.403)

The owner or operator of an aircraft is primarily responsible for maintaining an aircraft in an airworthy condition.

2. **What records or documents should be checked to determine that the owner or operator of an aircraft has complied with all required inspections and airworthiness directives?** (14 CFR 91.405)

The maintenance records (aircraft and engine logbooks). Each owner or operator of an aircraft shall ensure that maintenance personnel make appropriate entries in the aircraft maintenance records indicating the aircraft has been approved for return to service.

3. **What regulations apply concerning the operation of an aircraft that has had alterations or repairs which may have substantially affected its operation in flight?** (14 CFR 91.407)

No person may operate or carry passengers in any aircraft that has undergone maintenance, preventative maintenance, rebuilding, or alteration that may have appreciably changed its flight characteristics or substantially affected its operation in flight until an appropriately rated pilot with at least a private pilot certificate:

a. Flies the aircraft;

b. Makes an operational check of the maintenance performed or alteration made; and

c. Logs the flight in the aircraft records.

4. **Can you legally fly an aircraft that has an inoperative flap position indicator?**

Unless operations are conducted under 14 CFR §91.213, the regulations require that all equipment installed on an aircraft in compliance with either the Airworthiness Standards or the Operating Rules must be operative. If equipment originally installed in the aircraft is no longer operative, the Airworthiness Certificate is not valid until such equipment is either repaired or removed from that aircraft. *See next question for an exception.*

However, the rules also permit the publication of a Minimum Equipment List (MEL) where compliance with these equipment requirements is not necessary in the interest of safety under all conditions. Deviation from the equipment requirements of the regulation is maintained by alternate means. Experience has shown that with the various levels of redundancy designed into aircraft, operation of every system or component installed may not be necessary when the remaining operative equipment can provide an acceptable level of safety.

5. What responsibilities should a pilot be familiar with concerning inoperative equipment on the aircraft? (14 CFR 91.213)

a. No person may take off in an aircraft with inoperative instruments or equipment installed unless:
- An approved Minimum Equipment List exists for that aircraft;
- A letter of authorization from the FAA is carried within the aircraft authorizing use of a MEL; and
- The aircraft records available to the pilot must include an entry describing the inoperable instruments and equipment allowed by the MEL.

or:

b. A person may take off in an aircraft with inoperative instruments and equipment without an approved Minimum Equipment List provided:
- The flight operation is conducted in a non-turbine powered aircraft for which a Master Minimum Equipment List has not been developed; and
- The inoperable instruments and equipment are not part of the VFR-day type certification instruments and equipment prescribed in the applicable airworthiness regulations; and
- The inoperable instruments and equipment are removed from the aircraft, the cockpit control placarded, and the maintenance recorded; or the inoperable instruments and equipment are deactivated and placarded "Inoperative"; and
- A determination is made by a certificated, appropriately rated pilot or mechanic that the inoperative instruments or equipment do not constitute a hazard to the aircraft.

6. What are the required maintenance inspections for aircraft? (14 CFR 91.409)

No person may operate an aircraft unless, within the preceding 12 calendar months, it has had an annual inspection in accordance with 14 CFR Part 43 and has been approved for return to service. Also, no person may operate an aircraft carrying any person (other than a crewmember) for hire, and no person may give flight instruction for hire in an aircraft which that person provides, unless within the preceding 100 hours of time in service the aircraft has received an annual or 100-hour inspection and has been approved for return to service.

In summary, if the aircraft is operated for hire it must have a 100-hour inspection as well as an annual inspection when due. If not operated for hire, it must have an annual inspection only.

Note: Be capable of locating the 100-hour and annual inspections in the aircraft and engine logbooks.

7. How often must the transponder in an aircraft be tested and inspected? (14 CFR 91.413)

No person may use an ATC transponder unless it has been tested and inspected within the preceding 24 calendar months.

8. What responsibilities does an owner or operator have concerning maintenance records for their aircraft? (14 CFR 91.417)

Each registered owner or operator shall keep records of the maintenance, preventative maintenance, and alteration and records of the 100-hour, annual, progressive, and other required or approved inspections, as appropriate, for each aircraft (including the airframe) and each engine propeller, rotor and appliance of an aircraft. The records must include:

a. A description (or reference to data acceptable to the Administrator) of the work performed;

b. The date of completion of the work performed;

c. The signature and certificate number of the person approving the aircraft for return to service; and also

d. A record of the preventative maintenance must be entered in the maintenance records.

9. Define "preventative maintenance." (14 CFR Part 43)

Preventative maintenance items which can be performed by the pilot are listed in 14 CFR Part 43 and include such basic items as oil changes, wheel bearing lubrication, and hydraulic fluid (brakes, landing gear system) refills. However, even if Part 43 permits certain work, do not exceed your personal skill level.

10. What are "Special Flight Permits," and when are they necessary? (14 CFR 91.213, 14 CFR 21.197)

A Special Flight Permit may be issued for an aircraft that may not currently meet applicable airworthiness requirements but is capable of safe flight. These permits are typically issued for the following purposes:

a. Flying an aircraft to a base where repairs, alterations or maintenance are to be performed, or to a point of storage.

b. Delivering or exporting an aircraft.

c. Production flight testing new-production aircraft.

d. Evacuating aircraft from areas of impending danger.

e. Conducting customer demonstration flights in new-production aircraft that have satisfactorily completed production flight tests.

11. How are "Special Flight Permits" obtained? (FAA-H-8083-25)

If a special flight permit is needed, assistance and the necessary forms may be obtained from the local FSDO or Designated Airworthiness Representative (DAR).

12. What are "Airworthiness Directives" (ADs)? (FAA-H-8083-25)

An AD is the medium the FAA uses to notify aircraft owners and other potentially interested persons of unsafe conditions that may exist because of design defects, maintenance, or other causes, and to specify the conditions under which the product may continue to be operated. ADs are regulatory in nature, and compliance is mandatory. It is the aircraft owner's or operator's responsibility to ensure compliance with all pertinent ADs. ADs are divided into two categories: Those of an emergency nature requiring immediate compliance prior to further flight and those of a less urgent nature requiring compliance within a specified period of time. All ADs and the AD Biweekly are free on the Internet at **http://rgl.faa.gov**.

13. Are electronic flight bags (EFBs) approved for use as a replacement for paper reference material (POH & supplements, etc.) in the cockpit? (AC 91-78)

Yes; EFBs can be used during all phases of flight operations in lieu of paper reference material when the information displayed is the functional equivalent of the paper reference material replaced and is current, up-to-date, and valid. It is recommended that a secondary or back-up source of aeronautical information necessary for the flight be available.

E. Weather

1. List the effects of stable and unstable air on clouds, turbulence, precipitation and visibility. (AC 00-6A)

	Stable	*Unstable*
Clouds:	Stratiform	Cumuliform
Turbulence:	Smooth	Rough
Precipitation:	Steady	Showery
Visibility:	Fair to Poor	Good

2. What is the definition of the term "freezing level" and how can you determine where that level is? (AC 00-6A)

The freezing level is the lowest altitude in the atmosphere over a given location at which the air temperature reaches 0°C. It is possible to have multiple freezing layers when a temperature inversion occurs above the defined freezing level. A pilot should use icing forecasts as well as PIREPs to determine the approximate freezing level. Area forecasts, AIRMETs, SIGMETs, and low-level significant weather charts are examples of aviation weather products with icing information.

3. What conditions are necessary for structural icing to occur? (AC 00-6A)

Visible moisture and below freezing temperatures at the point moisture strikes the aircraft.

4. What action is recommended if you inadvertently encounter icing conditions? (AC 00-6A)

Change course and/or altitude; usually climb to a higher altitude, if possible.

5. Is frost considered a hazard to flight? Why? (AC 00-6A)

Yes, because even a small amount of frost on airfoils may prevent an aircraft from becoming airborne at normal takeoff speed. It is also possible that, once airborne, an aircraft could have insufficient margin of airspeed above stall so that moderate gusts or turning flight could produce incipient or complete stalling. Frost does not change the basic aerodynamics shape of the wing, but the roughness of its surface spoils the smooth flow of air, thus causing a slowing of airflow. This slowing of the air causes early airflow separation, resulting in a loss of lift.

6. What factors must be present for a thunderstorm to form? (AC 00-6A)

a. A source of lift (heating, fast-moving front)

b. Unstable air (nonstandard lapse rate)

c. High moisture content (temperature/dew point close)

7. Why is fog a major operational concern to pilots? (AC 00-6A)

It is of primary concern during takeoffs and landings. Fog can reduce vertical and horizontal visibilities to zero-zero. It can occur instantly from a clear condition, making takeoffs, landings, and even taxiing, potentially hazardous operations.

8. Why is wind shear an operational concern to pilots? (AC 00-6A)

Wind shear is an operational concern because unexpected changes in wind speed and direction can be potentially very hazardous to aircraft operations at low altitudes on approach to and departing from airports where your margin above stall is already small; wind shear can cause the airspeed to sink below the stall speed.

9. **What types of weather information will you examine to determine if wind shear conditions might affect your flight?** (AC 00-54)

   a. *Terminal forecasts* — any mention of low level wind shear (LLWS) or the possibility of severe thunderstorms, heavy rain showers, hail, and wind gusts suggest the potential for LLWS and microbursts.

   b. *METARs* — inspect for any indication of thunderstorms, rain showers, or blowing dust. Additional signs such as warming trends, gusty winds, cumulonimbus clouds, etc., should be noted.

   c. *Severe weather watch reports, SIGMETS, and convective SIGMETS* — severe convective weather is a prime source for wind shear and microbursts.

   d. *LLWAS (low level windshear alert system) reports* — installed at 110 airports in the U.S.; designed to detect wind shifts between outlying stations and a reference centerfield station.

   e. *PIREPs* — reports of sudden airspeed changes on departure or approach and landing corridors provide a real-time indication of the presence of wind shear.

F. Obtaining Weather Information

1. **What is the primary means of obtaining a weather briefing?** (AIM 7-1-2)

   The primary source is an individual briefing, tailored to your specific flight, obtained from a briefer at the AFSS/FSS. These briefings are available 24 hours a day by calling the toll-free number 1-800-WX-BRIEF.

2. **What types of weather briefings are available from an FSS briefer?** (AIM 7-1-4)

   Standard Briefing — Request anytime you are planning a flight and you have not received a previous briefing or have not received preliminary information through mass dissemination media (TIBS, DUAT, etc.).

   Continued

Abbreviated Briefing—Request when you need information to supplement mass disseminated data, update a previous briefing, or when you need only one or two items.

Outlook Briefing—Request whenever your proposed time of departure is six or more hours from the time of the briefing; for planning purposes only.

Inflight Briefing—Request when needed to update a preflight briefing.

G. Weather Reports, Forecasts and Charts

1. In METARs: (AC 00-45)

Visibilities are statute or nautical?

Statute

Cloud heights are AGL or MSL?

AGL

Wind directions are true or magnetic north?

True north

Wind speeds are knots or miles per hour?

Knots

2. Are the cloud bases and tops in PIREPs expressed in MSL or AGL? (AC 00-45)

MSL. Above sea level, the pilot reads MSL altitudes from the altimeter when making the report.

3. What are Terminal Aerodrome Forecasts (TAFs)? (AC 00-45)

Terminal Aerodrome Forecasts are for specific airports and cover an area within a 5-mile radius of the runway complex. They provide ceilings and visibilities, precipitation, and winds for times specified. They are issued four times daily and are valid for 24 hours.

4. What are Aviation Area Forecasts (FAs)? (AC 00-45)

Area Forecasts are comprised of four sections that provide forecasts of general weather conditions over a wide area (several states). They are used to determine forecast enroute weather and to interpolate conditions at an airport for which no TAF is issued. FAs are issued 3 times daily. All times are UTC (Universal Coordinated Time) in whole hours. Wind speed is in knots; wind direction, in degrees true. All distances except visibility are in nautical miles; visibility is in statute miles.

Each FA has the following sections:

a. Communications and product header sections

b. Precautionary statement section

c. A synopsis section

d. VFR clouds/wx section

5. What valuable information can be determined from winds and temperatures aloft forecasts? (AC 00-45)

Most favorable altitude — based on winds and direction of flight.

Areas of possible icing — by noting air temperatures of +2° to -20°C.

Temperature inversions.

Turbulence — by observing abrupt changes in wind direction and speed at different altitudes.

6. What is a SIGMET? (AC 00-45)

SIGMETs (Significant Meteorological Advisory) advise of weather potentially hazardous to all aircraft:

a. Severe icing not associated with a thunderstorm

b. Severe or extreme turbulence or clear air turbulence (CAT) not associated with thunderstorms

c. Widespread sand, duststorms or volcanic ash lowering visibilities to less than 3 miles

d. Volcanic ash

7. What is an AIRMET? (AC 00-45)

An AIRMET (Airman's Meteorological Advisory) is for weather that may be hazardous to single-engine and light aircraft:

a. Moderate icing

b. Moderate turbulence

c. Sustained winds at the surface of 30 knots or more

d. Widespread areas with visibilities below 3 miles and/or ceilings less than 1,000 feet

e. Extensive mountain obscurement

H. Aerodynamics

1. For what two reasons is load factor important to pilots? (FAA-H-8083-3)

a. Because of the obviously dangerous overload that is possible for a pilot to impose on the aircraft structure.

b. Because an increased load factor increases the stalling speed and makes stalls possible at seemingly safe flight speeds.

2. What situations may result in load factors reaching the maximum or being exceeded? (FAA-H-8083-3)

Level Turns—The load factor increases at a terrific rate after a bank has reached 45° or 50°. The load factor in a 60°-bank turn is 2 Gs. The load factor in a 80°-bank turn is 5.76 Gs. The wing must produce lift equal to these load factors if altitude is to be maintained.

Turbulence—Severe vertical gusts cause a sudden increase in angle of attack, resulting in large loads which are resisted by the inertia of the airplane.

Speed—The amount of excess load that can be imposed upon the wing depends on how fast the airplane is flying. At speeds below maneuvering speed, the airplane will stall before the load factor can become excessive. At speeds above maneuvering speed, the limit load factor for which an airplane is stressed can be exceeded by abrupt or excessive application of the controls or by strong turbulence.

3. What effect does an increase in load factor have on stalling speed? (FAA-H-8083-3)

As load factor increases, stalling speed increases. Load factor increases when an airplane follows a curved flight path, turns, pulls out from a dive, or a sudden or excessive application of back pressure is applied on the control wheel. Consequently, the stalling speed will also increase.

4. What causes an airplane to stall? (FAA-H-8083-3)

An airplane stalls when the critical angle of attack has been exceeded. When the angle of attack increases to approximately 18° to 20°, the air can no longer flow smoothly over the top wing surface. Because the airflow cannot make such great change in direction so quickly, it becomes impossible for the air to follow the contour of the wing. This is the stalling or critical angle of attack. This can occur at any airspeed, in any attitude, with any power setting.

5. What major problems can be caused by ground effect? (FAA-H-8083-3)

During landing, at a height of approximately one-tenth of a wing span above the surface, drag may be 40 percent less than when the airplane is operating out of ground effect. Therefore, any excess speed during the landing phase may result in a significant float distance. In such cases, if care is not exercised by the pilot, he/she may run out of runway and options at the same time.

During takeoff, due to the reduced drag in ground effect, the aircraft may seem capable of takeoff well below the recommended speed. However, as the airplane rises out of ground effect with a deficiency of speed, the greater induced drag may result in very marginal climb performance, or the inability of the airplane to fly at all. In extreme conditions, such as high temperature, high gross weight, and high density altitude, the airplane may become airborne initially with a deficiency of speed and then settle back to the runway.

I. Weight and Balance

1. What basic equation is used in all weight and balance problems to find the center of gravity location of an airplane and/or its components?

Weight x Arm = Moment

By rearrangement of this equation:
Weight = Moment/Arm
Arm (CG) = (Total) Moment/(Total) Weight

With any two known values, the third value can be found.

Remember: W A M (*Weight* x *Arm* = *Moment*)

2. What performance characteristics will be adversely affected when an aircraft has been overloaded? (FAA-H-8083-1)

a. Higher takeoff speed
b. Longer takeoff run
c. Reduced rate and angle of climb
d. Lower maximum altitude
e. Shorter range
f. Reduced cruising speed
g. Reduced maneuverability
h. Higher stall speed
i. Higher landing speed
j. Longer landing roll
k. Excessive weight on the nosewheel

3. What effect does a forward center of gravity have on an aircraft's flight characteristics? (FAA-H-8083-3)

Higher stall speed—stalling angle of attack is reached at a higher speed due to increased wing loading.

Slower cruise speed—increased drag; greater angle of attack is required to maintain altitude.

More stable—the center of gravity is farther forward from the center of pressure which increases longitudinal stability.

Greater back elevator pressure required—longer takeoff roll; higher approach speeds and problems with landing flare.

4. What effect does a rearward center of gravity have on an aircraft's flight characteristics? (FAA-H-8083-3)

Lower stall speed—less wing loading.

Higher cruise speed—reduced drag; smaller angle of attack is required to maintain altitude.

Less stable—stall and spin recovery more difficult; the center of gravity is closer to the center of pressure, causing longitudinal instability.

5. What is the weight of aircraft fuel and oil? (FAA-H-8083-25)

Aircraft fuel weighs 6 pounds per gallon. Aircraft oil weighs 7.5 pounds per gallon.

J. Aircraft Performance

1. How does weight affect takeoff and landing performance? (FAA-H-8083-3)

Increased gross weight can have a significant effect on takeoff performance:

a. Higher liftoff speed;

b. Greater mass to accelerate (slow acceleration);

c. Increased retarding force (drag and ground friction); and

d. Longer takeoff distance.

The effect of gross weight on landing distance is that the airplane will require a greater speed to support the airplane at the landing angle of attack and lift coefficient resulting in an increased landing distance.

2. How does air density affect takeoff and landing performance? (FAA-H-8083-3)

An increase in density altitude (decrease in air density) can also have the following effects on takeoff performance:

a. Greater takeoff speed required;

b. Decreased thrust and reduced acceleration;

c. Longer takeoff ground roll; and

d. Decreased climb rate.

An increase in density altitude (decrease in air density) will increase the landing ground speed but will not alter the net retarding force. Thus, the airplane will land at the same indicated airspeed as normal but because of reduced air density the true airspeed will be greater. This will result in a longer minimum landing distance.

3. Know the following speeds for your airplane:

V_{SO}: _____ Stall speed in landing configuration; the calibrated power-off stalling speed or the minimum steady flight speed at which the airplane is controllable in the landing configuration.

V_{S1}: _____ Stall speed clean or in specified configuration; the calibrated power-off stalling speed or the minimum steady speed at which the airplane is controllable in a specified configuration.

V_Y: _____ Best rate-of-climb speed; the calibrated airspeed at which the airplane will obtain the maximum increase in altitude per unit of time. This best rate-of-climb speed normally decreases slightly with altitude.

V_X: _____ Best angle-of-climb speed; the calibrated airspeed at which the airplane will obtain the highest altitude in a given horizontal distance. This best angle-of-climb speed normally increases with altitude.

V_{LE}: _____ Maximum landing gear extension speed; the maximum calibrated airspeed at which the airplane can be safely flown with the landing gear extended. This is a problem involving stability and controllability.

V_{LO}: _____ Maximum landing gear operating speed; the maximum calibrated airspeed at which the landing gear can be safely extended or retracted. This is a problem involving the airloads imposed on the operating mechanism during extension or retraction of the gear.

V_{FE}: _____ Maximum flap extension speed; the highest calibrated airspeed permissible with the wing flaps in a prescribed extended position. This is a problem involving the airloads imposed on the structure of the flaps.

V_A: _____ Maneuvering speed; the calibrated design maneuvering airspeed. This is the maximum speed at which the limit load can be imposed (either by gusts or full deflection of the control surfaces) without causing structural damage.

V_{NO}: _____ Normal operating speed; the maximum calibrated airspeed for normal operation or the maximum structural cruise speed. This is the speed above which exceeding the limit load factor may cause permanent deformation of the airplane structure.

V_{NE}: _____ Never exceed speed; the calibrated airspeed which should never be exceeded. If flight is attempted above this speed, structural damage or structural failure may result.

4. **The following questions are designed to provide the pilot with a general review of the basic information they should know about their specific airplane before taking a flight check or review.**

   a. What is the normal climb-out speed?

   b. What is the normal approach-to-land speed?

   c. What is red-line speed?

   d. What engine-out glide speed will give you maximum range?

   e. What is the make and horsepower of the engine?

   f. How many usable gallons of fuel can you carry?

   g. Where are the fuel tanks located and what are their capacities?

   h. What is the octane rating of the fuel used by your aircraft?

   i. How do you drain the fuel sumps?

   j. What are the minimum and maximum oil capacities?

   k. What weight of oil is being used?

Continued

l. What is the maximum oil temperature and pressure?

m. Is the landing gear fixed, manual, hydraulic or electric?
If retractable, what is the backup system for lowering the gear?

n. What is the maximum demonstrated crosswind component for the aircraft?

o. How many people will this aircraft carry safely with a full fuel load?

p. What is the maximum allowable weight the aircraft can carry with baggage in the baggage compartment?

q. What takeoff distance is required if a takeoff were made from a sea-level pressure altitude?

r. What is your maximum allowable useful load?

s. Solve a weight and balance problem for the flight you plan to make with one passenger at 170 pounds.
   • Does your load fall within the weight and balance envelope?
   • What is the final gross weight?
   • How much fuel can be carried?
   • How much baggage can be carried with full fuel?

t. Know the function of the various types of antennae on your aircraft.

K. Navigation

1. What type of aeronautical charts are available for use in VFR navigation? (AIM 9-1-4)

a. *Sectional Charts*—designed for visual navigation of slow to medium speed aircraft. One inch equals 6.86 nautical miles. They are revised semiannually, except most Alaskan charts which are revised annually.

b. *VFR Terminal Area Charts (TAC)*—TACs depict the Class B airspace. While similar to sectional charts, TACs have more detail because the scale is larger. One inch equals 3.43 nautical miles. Charts are revised semiannually, except in Puerto Rico and the Virgin Islands where they are revised annually.

c. *World Aeronautical Charts (WAC)*—WACs cover land areas for navigation by moderate speed aircraft operating at high altitudes. Because of a smaller scale, WACs do not show as much detail as sectionals or TACs, and therefore are not recommended for pilots of low speed, low altitude aircraft. One inch equals 13.7 nautical miles. WACs are revised annually except for a few in Alaska and the Caribbean, which are revised biennially.

d. *VFR Flyway Planning Charts*—This chart is printed on the reverse side of selected TAC charts. The coverage is the same as the associated TAC. They depict flight paths and altitudes recommended for use to bypass high traffic areas.

2. What is "magnetic variation"? (FAA-H-8083-25)

Magnetic variation is the error induced by the difference in location of true north and magnetic north. It is expressed in east or west variation.

3. How do you convert a true direction to a magnetic direction? (FAA-H-8083-25)

To convert from TRUE (measured from the meridians on the chart) to MAGNETIC, note the variation shown by the nearest isogonic line. If variation is west, add; if east, subtract.

Remember: East is Least (Subtract)
West is Best (Add)

4. What is "magnetic deviation"? (FAA-H-8083-25)

Because of magnetic influences within the airplane itself (electrical circuits, radios, lights, tools, engine, magnetized metal parts, etc.) the compass needle is frequently deflected from its normal reading. This deflection is called deviation. Deviation is different for each airplane, and also varies for different headings of the same airplane. The deviation value may be found on a deviation card located in the airplane.

L. Cross-Country Flying

1. Flight log example, VFR flight plan:

Careful preflight planning is extremely important. A wise pilot ensures a successful cross-country flight by getting a good weather briefing and completing a flight log before flight.

a. Get a weather briefing from a Flight Service Station. Write it down.

b. Draw course lines and mark checkpoints on the chart.

c. Enter checkpoints on the log.

d. Enter NAVAIDs on the log.

e. Enter VOR courses on the log.

f. Enter altitude on the log.

g. Enter the wind (direction/speed) and temperature on the log.

h. Measure the true course on the chart and enter it on the log.

i. Compute the true airspeed and enter it on the log.

j. Compute the WCA and GS and enter them on the log.

k. Determine variation from chart and enter it on the log.

l. Determine deviation from compass correction card and enter it on the log.

m. Measure distances on the chart and enter them on the log.

n. Figure ETE and ETA and enter them on the log.

o. Calculate fuel burn and usage; enter them on the log.

p. Compute weight and balance.

q. Compute takeoff and landing performance.

r. Complete a Flight Plan form.

s. File a Flight Plan with FSS.

2. Diversion to Alternate/Lost Procedures:

What actions should be taken if you become disoriented or lost on a cross-country flight?

Condition I: plenty of fuel and weather conditions good.

a. Straighten up and fly right. Fly a specific heading in a direction you believe to be correct (or circle, if unsure); don't wander aimlessly.

b. If you have been flying a steady compass heading and keeping a relatively accurate navigation log, it's not likely you will have a problem locating your position.

c. If several VORs are within reception distance, use them for a cross-bearing to determine position (even a single VOR can be enormous help in narrowing down your possible position); or, fly to the station—there's no doubt where you are then.

d. Use knowledge of your last known position, elapsed time, approximate wind direction and ground speed, to establish how far you may have traveled since your last checkpoint.

e. Use this distance as a radius and draw a semicircle ahead of your last known position on chart. For example, you estimate your ground speed at 120 knots. If you have been flying 20 minutes since your last checkpoint, then the no-wind radius of your semicircle is 40 miles projected along the direction of your estimated track.

f. If still unsure of your position, loosen up the eyeballs and start some first-class pilotage. Look for something big. Don't concern yourself with the minute or trivial at this point. Often, there will be linear features such as rivers, mountain ranges, or prominent highways and railroads that are easy to identify. You can use them simply as references for orientation purposes and thus find them of great value in fixing your approximate position.

Continued

Condition II: low on fuel; weather deteriorating; inadequate experience; darkness imminent; and/or equipment malfunctioning.

Get it on the ground! Most accidents are the product of mistakes which have multiplied over a period of time and getting lost is no exception: don't push your luck. It may well be that in doing so, you have added the final mistake which will add another figure to the accident statistics. If terrain or other conditions make landing impossible at the moment, don't waste time, for it is of the essence: don't search for the perfect field—anything usable will do. Remember, most people on the ground know where they are, and you know that you do not.

3. If it becomes apparent that you cannot locate your position, what action is recommended at this point?

The FAA recommends the use of the "4 Cs":

a. Climb—The higher altitude allows better communication capability as well as better visual range for identification of landmarks.

b. Communicate—Use the system. Use 121.5 MHz if no other frequency produced results. It is guarded by FSS's, control towers, military towers, approach control facilities, and Air Route Traffic Control Centers.

c. Confess—Once communications are established, let them know your problem.

d. Comply—Follow instructions.

4. What is "DF guidance"? (AIM Glossary)

Available in Alaska, DF guidance is given to aircraft in distress or to other aircraft that request the service. Headings are provided to the aircraft by facilities equipped with direction finding equipment. Following these headings will lead the aircraft to a predetermined point such as the DF station or an airport. DF guidance for practice is provided when workload permits.

5. **While en route on a cross-country flight, weather has deteriorated and it becomes necessary to divert to an alternate airport. What is the recommended procedure?**

   a. Mark your present position on the chart. It is also advisable to write the current time next to this mark.

   b. Establish a general direction to the alternate and turn to it immediately.

   c. As time permits, determine distance, ground speed, and estimated time en route to the alternate.

M. Radio Communications

1. **What is the universal VHF "Emergency" frequency?** (AIM 6-3-1)

   121.5 MHz; this frequency is guarded by military towers, most civil towers, flight service stations, and radar facilities.

2. **If operating into an airport without an operating control tower, FSS or UNICOM, what procedure should be followed?** (AIM 4-1-9)

   A pilot should monitor the "multicom" frequency of 122.9 when approaching the airport and broadcast intentions when approximately five miles out. Multicom is a mobile service not open to public use, used to provide communications essential to conduct the activities being performed by or directed from private aircraft.

3. **What are the standard Flight Service Station frequencies?** (AIM 4-2-14)

   121.5 for emergencies, 122.0 for flight watch, and 122.2 for other communications are normally available at all FSS's. Other frequencies at controlling FSS's may be available determined by altitude and terrain. Consult the Airport/Facility Directory for complete information.

4. What is "Local Airport Advisory Service"? (AIM 4-1-9)

Certain FSS's provide Local Airport Advisory service to pilots when an FSS is physically located on an airport that doesn't have a control tower or where the tower is operated on a part-time basis. The CTAF (usually 123.6) for FSS's that provide this service will be disseminated in appropriate aeronautical publications. A CTAF FSS provides wind direction and speed, NOTAMs, taxi routes, traffic pattern information, and instrument approach procedures. The information is advisory in nature and does not constitute an ATC clearance.

5. Are electronic flight bags (EFBs) approved for use as a replacement for paper reference material (POH & supplements, etc.) in the cockpit? (AC 91-78)

Yes; EFBs can be used during all phases of flight operations in lieu of paper reference material when the information displayed is the functional equivalent of the paper reference material replaced and is current, up-to-date, and valid. It is recommended that a secondary or back-up source of aeronautical information necessary for the flight be available.

N. Federal Aviation Regulations Part 91

1. If an in-flight emergency requires immediate action by the pilot, what authority and responsibilities does he/she have? (14 CFR 91.3)

a. The pilot-in-command is directly responsible for and is the final authority as to the operation of an aircraft.

b. The pilot-in-command may deviate from any regulation to the extent necessary in dealing with the emergency.

c. A pilot-in-command who deviates from a regulation to meet an emergency must send a written report to the FAA if so requested.

2. What restrictions apply to pilots concerning the use of drugs and alcohol? (14 CFR 91.17)

No person may act or attempt to act as a crewmember of a civil aircraft:

a. within 8 hours after the consumption of any alcoholic beverage;

b. while under the influence of alcohol;

c. while having .04 percent by weight or more alcohol in the blood;

d. while using any drug that affects the person's faculties in any way contrary to safety.

3. Is it permissible for a pilot to allow a person who is obviously under the influence of intoxicating liquors or drugs to be carried aboard an aircraft? (14 CFR 91.17)

No. Except in an emergency, no pilot of a civil aircraft may allow a person who appears to be intoxicated or who demonstrates by manner or physical indications that the individual is under the influence of drugs (except a medical patient under proper care) to be carried in that aircraft.

4. Concerning a flight in the local area, is any preflight action required, and if so, what must it consist of? (14 CFR 91.103)

Yes. Pilots must familiarize themselves with all available information concerning that flight, including runway lengths at airports of intended use, and takeoff and landing distance data under existing conditions.

5. Preflight action as required by regulation for all flights away from the vicinity of the departure airport shall include a review of what specific information? (14 CFR 91.103)

For a flight under IFR or a flight not in the vicinity of an airport:

a. Weather reports and forecasts.

b. Fuel requirements.

c. Alternatives available if the planned flight cannot be completed.

d. Any known traffic delays of which the pilot-in-command has been advised by ATC.

e. Runway lengths of intended use.

f. Takeoff and landing distance data.

6. Which persons on board an aircraft are required to use seatbelts and when? (14 CFR 91.107)

During takeoff and landing, each person on board an aircraft must occupy a seat or berth with a safety belt and shoulder harness, if installed, properly secured about him/her. However, a person who has not reached his or her second birthday may be held by an adult who is occupying a seat or a berth, and a person on board for the purpose of engaging in sport parachuting may use the floor of the aircraft as a seat.

7. If operating an aircraft in close proximity to another, such as formation flight, what regulations apply? (14 CFR 91.111)

a. No person may operate an aircraft so close to another aircraft as to create a collision hazard.

b. No person may operate an aircraft in formation flight except by arrangement with the pilot-in-command of each aircraft in the formation.

c. No person may operate an aircraft carrying passengers for hire in formation flight.

8. What is the order of right-of-way as applied to the different categories of aircraft? (14 CFR 91.113)

a. A balloon has the right-of-way over any other category of aircraft.

b. A glider has the right-of way over an airship, powered parachute, weight-shift control aircraft, airplane, or rotorcraft.

c. An airship has the right-of-way over a powered parachute, weight-shift control aircraft, airplane, or rotorcraft.

Aircraft towing or refueling other aircraft have the right-of-way over all other engine-driven aircraft.

9. When would an aircraft have the right-of-way over all other air traffic? (14 CFR 91.113)

An aircraft in distress has the right-of-way over all other air traffic.

10. State the required action for each of the aircraft confrontations: Converging, Approaching head-on, Overtaking. (14 CFR 91.113)

Converging: aircraft on right has the right-of-way if same category. Otherwise, see Question 8.

Approaching head-on: both aircraft shall alter course to right.

Overtaking: aircraft being overtaken has the right-of-way; pilot of the overtaking aircraft shall alter course to the right.

11. What right-of-way rules apply when two or more aircraft are approaching an airport for the purpose of landing? (14 CFR 91.113)

Aircraft on final approach to land or while landing have the right-of-way over aircraft in flight or operating on the surface, except that they shall not take advantage of this rule to force an aircraft off the runway surface which has already landed and is attempting to make way for an aircraft on final approach. When two or more aircraft are approaching an airport for the purpose of landing, the aircraft at the lower altitude has the right-of-way, but it shall not take advantage of this rule to cut in front of another which is on final approach to land or to overtake that aircraft.

12. Unless otherwise authorized or required by ATC, what is the maximum indicated airspeed at which a person may operate an aircraft below 10,000 feet MSL? (14 CFR 91.117)

No person may operate an aircraft below 10,000 feet MSL at an indicated airspeed of more than 250 knots (288 mph).

13. What is the minimum safe altitude that an aircraft may be operated over a congested area of a city? (14 CFR 91.119)

Except when necessary for takeoff or landing, no person may operate an aircraft over a congested area of a city, town, or settlement, or over any open-air assembly of persons, below an altitude of 1,000 feet above the highest obstacle within a horizontal radius of 2,000 feet of the aircraft.

14. In areas other than congested areas, what minimum safe altitudes shall be used? (14 CFR 91.119)

Except when necessary for takeoff or landing, an aircraft shall be operated no lower than 500 feet above the surface, except over open water or sparsely populated areas. In those cases, the aircraft may not be operated closer than 500 feet to any person, vessel, vehicle or structure.

15. When flying below 18,000 feet MSL, cruising altitude must be maintained by reference to an altimeter set using what procedure? (14 CFR 91.121)

When the barometric pressure is 31.00" Hg or less, each person operating an aircraft shall maintain the cruising altitude or flight level of that aircraft, as the case may be, by reference to an altimeter set to the current reported altimeter setting of a station along the route and within 100 nautical miles of the aircraft. If there is no station within this area, the current reported altimeter setting of an available station may be used. If the barometric pressure exceeds 31.00" Hg, consult the *Aeronautical Information Manual* for correct procedures.

16. If an altimeter setting is not available before flight, what procedure should be used? (14 CFR 91.121)

Use the same procedure as in the case of an aircraft not equipped with a radio: the elevation of the departure airport or an appropriate altimeter setting available before departure should be used.

17. When may a pilot intentionally deviate from an ATC clearance or instruction? (14 CFR 91.123)

No pilot may deviate from an ATC clearance unless an amended clearance has been obtained, an emergency exists, or if the pilot is acting in response to a traffic and collision avoidance system resolution advisory.

18. As pilot-in-command, what action, if any, is required of you if you deviate from an ATC instruction and priority is given? (14 CFR 91.123)

Two actions are required of you as PIC:

a. Each pilot-in-command who, in an emergency, deviates from an ATC clearance or instruction shall notify ATC of that deviation as soon as possible (in-the-air responsibility).

b. Each pilot-in-command who is given priority by ATC in an emergency shall submit a detailed report of that emergency within 48 hours to the manager of that ATC facility, if requested by ATC (on-the-ground responsibility).

19. In the event of radio failure while operating at tower controlled airports within Class B, C, or D airspace, what are the different types and meanings of light gun signals you might receive from an ATC tower? (14 CFR 91.125)

Light	*On Ground*	*In Air*
Steady green	Cleared for takeoff	Cleared to land
Flashing green	Cleared to taxi	Return for landing
Steady red	Stop	Yield, continue circling
Flashing red	Taxi clear of runway	Unsafe, do not land
Flashing white	Return to start	Not used
Alternating red/green	Exercise extreme caution	Exercise extreme caution

20. What general rules apply concerning traffic pattern operations at non-tower airports within Class E or G airspace? (14 CFR 91.126, 91.127)

Each person operating an aircraft to or from an airport without an operating control tower shall:

a. In the case of an airplane approaching to land, make all turns of that airplane to the left unless the airport displays approved light signals or visual markings indicating that turns should be made to the right, in which case the pilot shall make all turns to the right.

b. In the case of an aircraft departing an airport, comply with any traffic patterns established for that airport in Part 93.

21. What procedure should be used when approaching to land on a runway with a Visual Approach Slope Indicator? (14 CFR 91.129)

Aircraft approaching to land on a runway served by a Visual Approach Slope Indicator shall maintain an altitude at or above the glide slope until a lower altitude is necessary for a safe landing.

22. What is the fuel requirement for VFR flight at night? (14 CFR 91.151)

No person may begin a flight in an airplane under VFR conditions unless (considering wind and forecast weather conditions) there is enough fuel to fly to the first point of intended landing and, assuming normal cruising speed, at night, fly after that for at least 45 minutes.

23. What is the fuel requirement for VFR flight during the day? (14 CFR 91.151)

During the day, you must be able to fly to the first point of intended landing, and assuming normal cruising speed, fly after that for at least 30 minutes.

24. When operating an aircraft under VFR in level cruising flight at an altitude of more than 3,000 feet above the surface, what rules apply concerning specific altitudes flown? (14 CFR 91.159)

When operating above 3,000 feet AGL but less than 18,000 feet MSL on a *magnetic course* of 0° to 179°, fly at an odd-thousand-foot MSL altitude plus 500 feet. When on a *magnetic course* of 180° to 359°, fly at an even-thousand-foot MSL altitude plus 500 feet.

25. What instruments and equipment are required for VFR day flight? (14 CFR 91.205)

For VFR flight during the day, the following instruments and equipment are required:

a. Airspeed indicator

b. Altimeter

c. Magnetic direction indicator compass

d. Tachometer for each engine

e. Oil pressure gauge for each engine

f. Temperature gauge for each liquid-cooled engine

g. Oil temperature gauge for each air-cooled engine

h. Manifold pressure gauge for each altitude engine

i. Fuel gauge indicating the quantity in each tank

j. Landing gear position indicator

k. Flotation gear (if operated for hire over water beyond power-off gliding distance from shore)

l. Safety belts (approved metal-to-metal latching device for each occupant over 2 years old)

m. Shoulder harnesses (for each front seat if aircraft manufactured after 1978)

n. Emergency locator transmitter

26. What instruments and equipment are required for VFR night flight? (14 CFR 91.205)

For VFR flight at night, the following instruments and equipment are required:

a. Instruments and equipment required for VFR day flight;

b. Approved position lights (navigation lights);

c. An approved aviation red or aviation white anticollision light system;

d. If the aircraft is operated for hire, one electric landing light;

e. An adequate source of electrical energy for all installed electrical and radio equipment; and

f. One spare set of fuses, or three spare fuses of each kind required, that are accessible to the pilot in flight.

27. Is an emergency locator transmitter (ELT) required on all aircraft? (14 CFR 91.207)

No person may operate a U.S.-registered civil airplane unless there is attached to the airplane an automatic-type emergency locator transmitter that is in operable condition. Several exceptions exist, including the following:

a. Aircraft engaged in training operations conducted entirely within a 50-nautical-mile radius of the airport from which such local flight operations began.

b. Aircraft engaged in design and testing.

c. New aircraft engaged in manufacture, preparation and delivery.

d. Aircraft engaged in agricultural operations.

28. When must the batteries in an emergency locator transmitter be replaced or recharged, if rechargeable? (14 CFR 91.207)

Batteries used in ELTs must be replaced (or recharged, if the batteries are rechargeable):

a. When the transmitter has been in use for more than 1 cumulative hour; or

b. When 50 percent of their useful life (or, if rechargeable batteries, 50 percent of their useful life of charge), has expired.

29. When must the required position lights be on? (14 CFR 91.209)

Aircraft position lights must be on during operations from sunset to sunrise.

30. What are the regulations concerning use of supplemental oxygen on board an aircraft? (14 CFR 91.211)

a. At cabin pressure altitudes above 12,500 feet MSL up to and including 14,000 feet MSL: for that part of the flight at those altitudes that is more than 30 minutes, the required minimum flight crew must be provided with and use supplemental oxygen.

b. At cabin pressure altitudes above 14,000 feet MSL up to and including 15,000 feet MSL: for the entire flight time at those altitudes, the required flight crew is provided with and uses supplemental oxygen.

c. At cabin pressure altitudes above 15,000 feet MSL: each occupant is provided with supplemental oxygen.

31. According to regulations, where is aerobatic flight of an aircraft not permitted? (14 CFR 91.303)

No person may operate an aircraft in aerobatic flight:

a. Over any congested area of city, town, or settlement;

b. Over an open air assembly of persons;

c. Within the lateral boundaries of the surface areas of Class B, Class C, Class D, Class E airspace designated for an airport;

d. Within 4 nautical miles of the center line of a Federal airway;

e. Below an altitude of 1,500 feet above the surface; or

f. When flight visibility is less than 3 statute miles.

32. Define aerobatic flight. (14 CFR 91.303)

Aerobatic flight means an intentional maneuver involving an abrupt change in an aircraft's attitude, an abnormal attitude, or abnormal acceleration, not necessary for normal flight.

33. When are parachutes required on board an aircraft? (14 CFR 91.307)

a. Unless each occupant of the aircraft is wearing an approved parachute, no pilot of a civil aircraft carrying any person (other than a crewmember) may execute any intentional maneuver that exceeds:
   • A bank angle of 60° relative to the horizon; or
   • A nose-up or nose-down attitude of 30° relative to the horizon.

b. The above regulation does not apply to:
   • Flight tests for pilot certification or rating; or
   • Spins and other flight maneuvers required by the regulations for any certificate or rating when given by a flight instructor or ATP instructing in accordance with 14 CFR §61.169.

O. Airspace

1. What is Class A airspace? (AIM 3-2-2)

Generally, that airspace from 18,000 feet MSL up to and including FL600, including that airspace overlying the waters within 12 nautical miles of the coast of the 48 contiguous states and Alaska; and designated international airspace beyond 12 nautical miles of the coast of the 48 contiguous states and Alaska within areas of domestic radio navigational signal or ATC radar coverage, and within which domestic procedures are applied.

2. Can a flight under VFR be conducted within Class A airspace? (14 CFR 91.135)

No. Unless otherwise authorized by ATC, each person operating an aircraft in Class A airspace must operate that aircraft under instrument flight rules (IFR).

3. What is the minimum pilot certification for operations conducted within Class A airspace? (14 CFR 91.135)

The pilot must be at least a private pilot with an instrument rating.

4. What minimum equipment is required for flight operations within Class A airspace? (14 CFR 91.135)

a. A two-way radio capable of communicating with ATC on the frequency assigned.

b. A Mode C altitude encoding transponder.

c. Instruments and equipment required for IFR operations.

5. How is Class A airspace depicted on navigation charts? (AIM 3-2-2)

Class A airspace is not specifically charted.

6. What is the definition of Class B airspace? (AIM 3-2-3)

Generally, that airspace from the surface to 10,000 feet MSL surrounding the nation's busiest airports in terms of IFR operations or passenger enplanements. The configuration of each Class B airspace area is individually tailored and consists of a surface area and two or more layers (some Class B airspace areas resemble upside-down wedding cakes), and is designated to contain all published instrument procedures once an aircraft enters the airspace.

7. What minimum pilot certification is required to operate an aircraft within Class B airspace? (14 CFR 91.131)

No person may take off or land a civil aircraft at an airport within a Class B airspace area or operate a civil aircraft within a Class B airspace area unless:

a. In order to take off or land at an airport within Class B airspace, including the primary airport, a pilot must hold at least a private pilot certificate or be a student or recreational pilot who has met the requirements of 14 CFR §61.95 (Operations in Class B airspace and at airports located with Class B airspace).

b. Certain Class B airspace areas do not allow student pilot operations to be conducted to or from the primary airport, unless the pilot-in-command holds at least a private pilot certificate (example: Dallas/Fort Worth International).

8. What is the minimum equipment required for operations of an aircraft within Class B airspace? (14 CFR 91.131)

a. An operable two-way radio capable of communications with ATC on the appropriate frequencies for that area.

b. A Mode C altitude encoding transponder.

c. If IFR, a VOR is also required.

9. Before operating an aircraft into Class B airspace, what basic requirement must be met? (14 CFR 91.131)

Arriving aircraft must obtain an ATC clearance from the ATC facility having jurisdiction for that area prior to operating an aircraft in that area.

10. What minimum weather conditions are required when conducting VFR flight operations within Class B airspace? (14 CFR 91.155)

VFR flight operations must be conducted clear of clouds with at least 3 statute miles flight visibility.

11. How is Class B airspace depicted on navigational charts? (AIM 3-2-3)

Class B airspace is charted on Sectional Charts, IFR En Route Low Altitude Charts, and Terminal Area Charts. A solid shaded blue line depicts the lateral limits of Class B airspace. The base and ceiling of the airspace is shown with one number over another, i.e., 100/25.

12. What basic ATC services are provided to all aircraft operating within Class B airspace? (AIM 3-2-3)

VFR pilots will be provided sequencing and separation from other aircraft while operating within Class B airspace.

13. It becomes apparent that wake turbulence may be encountered while ATC is providing sequencing and separation services in Class B airspace. Whose responsibility is it to avoid this turbulence? (AIM 3-2-3)

The pilot-in-command is responsible. These services provided by ATC do not relieve pilots of their responsibilities to see and avoid other traffic operating in basic VFR weather conditions, to adjust their operations and flight path as necessary to preclude serious wake turbulence encounters or to maintain appropriate terrain and obstruction clearance.

14. What is the maximum speed an aircraft may be operated within Class B airspace? (14 CFR 91.117)

Unless otherwise authorized by the Administrator (or by ATC), no person may operate an aircraft below 10,000 feet MSL at an indicated airspeed of more than 250 knots (288 mph).

15. When operating beneath the lateral limits of Class B airspace, or in a VFR corridor designated through Class B airspace, what maximum speed is authorized? (14 CFR 91.117)

No person may operate an aircraft in the airspace underlying a Class B airspace area or in a VFR corridor designated through such a Class B airspace area, at an indicated airspeed of more than 200 knots (230 mph).

16. What is Class C airspace? (AIM 3-2-4)

Generally, that airspace from the surface to 4,000 feet above the airport elevation (charted in MSL) surrounding those airports that have an operational control tower, are serviced by a radar approach control, and that have a certain number of IFR operations or passenger enplanements.

17. What are the basic dimensions of Class C airspace? (AIM 3-2-4)

Although the configuration of each Class C airspace area is individually tailored, the airspace usually consists of two circles both centered on the primary airport for the Class C airspace. The surface area has a radius of 5 NM. The shelf area has a radius of 10 NM. The airspace of the inner circle extends from the surface up to 4,000 feet above the airport. The airspace area between the 5 and 10 NM rings begin at a height 1,200 feet AGL and extends to the same altitude cap as the surface area. The outer area consists of airspace beginning at 10 NM extending to a radius of 20 NM from the primary airport and extends from the lower limits of radar/radio coverage up to the ceiling of the approach controls delegated airspace.

18. What minimum pilot certification is required to operate an aircraft within Class C airspace? (AIM 3-2-4)

A student pilot certificate.

19. What minimum equipment is required to operate an aircraft within Class C airspace? (14 CFR 91.130, 91.215)

Unless otherwise authorized by the ATC having jurisdiction over the Class C airspace area, no person may operate an aircraft within a Class C airspace area unless that aircraft is equipped with the following:

a. A two-way radio

b. Automatic pressure altitude reporting equipment having Mode C capability

20. When operating an aircraft through Class C airspace or to an airport within Class C airspace, what basic requirement must be met? (14 CFR 91.130)

Each person must establish two-way radio communications with the ATC facilities providing air traffic service prior to entering that airspace and thereafter maintain those communications while within that airspace.

21. Two-way radio communications must be "established" prior to entering Class C airspace. Define the term "established." (AIM 3-2-4)

If a controller responds to a radio call with, "(aircraft call sign) standby," radio communications have been established. It is important to understand that if the controller responds to the initial radio call *without* using the aircraft identification, radio communications have *not* been established and the pilot may not enter the Class C airspace.

22. When departing a satellite airport without an operative control tower located within Class C airspace, what requirement must be met? (14 CFR 91.130)

Each person must establish and maintain two-way radio communications with the ATC facilities having jurisdiction over the Class C airspace area as soon as practicable after departing.

23. What minimum weather conditions are required when conducting VFR flight operations within Class C airspace? (14 CFR 91.155)

VFR flight operations within Class C airspace require 3 statute miles flight visibility and cloud clearances of at least 500 feet below, 1,000 feet above and 2,000 feet horizontal to clouds.

24. How is Class C airspace depicted on navigational charts? (AIM 3-2-4)

A solid magenta line is used to depict Class C airspace. Class C airspace is charted on Sectional Charts, IFR En Route Low Altitude, and Terminal Area Charts where appropriate.

25. What type of Air Traffic Control services are provided when operating within Class C airspace? (AIM 3-2-4)

When two-way communications and radar contact are established within Class C airspace or the Outer Area, participating VFR aircraft will be provided with:

a. Sequencing to the primary airport.

b. Separation from all IFR aircraft.

26. Describe the various types of terminal radar services available for VFR aircraft. (AIM 4-1-18)

Basic radar service—Safety alerts, traffic advisories, limited radar vectoring (on a workload-permitting basis) and sequencing at locations where procedures have been established for this purpose and/or when covered by a letter of agreement.

TRSA service—Radar sequencing and separation service for VFR aircraft in a TRSA.

Class C service—This service provides, in addition to basic radar service, approved separation between IFR and VFR aircraft, and sequencing of VFR arrivals to the primary airport.

Class B service—Provides, in addition to basic radar service, approved separation of aircraft based on IFR, VFR, and/or weight, and sequencing of VFR arrivals to the primary airport(s).

27. Where is Mode C altitude encoding transponder equipment required? (14 CFR 91.215)

a. In Class A, Class B, and Class C airspace areas.

b. In all airspace within a 30-mile radius of the primary airport for which a Class B airspace area has been designated, from the surface to 10,000 feet MSL.

c. In all airspace above the ceiling and within the lateral boundaries of a Class C airspace area designated for an airport upward to 10,000 feet MSL.

d. In all airspace of the 48 contiguous states and the District of Columbia at and above 10,000 feet MSL, excluding the airspace at and below 2,500 feet above the surface.

e. In the airspace from the surface to 10,000 feet MSL within a 10 nautical mile radius of designated airport, excluding that airspace below 1,200 feet AGL outside of the lateral boundaries.

28. What is the maximum speed an aircraft may be operated within Class C airspace? (14 CFR 91.117)

Unless otherwise authorized or required by ATC, no person may operate an aircraft at or below 2,500 feet above the surface within 4 nautical miles of the primary airport of a Class C or Class D airspace area at an indicated speed of more than 200 knots (230 mph).

29. What is Class D airspace? (AIM 3-2-5)

Generally, that airspace from the surface to 2,500 feet above the airport elevation (charted in MSL) surrounding those airports that have an operational control tower. The configuration of each Class D airspace area is individually tailored and when instrument procedures are published, the airspace will normally be designed to contain those procedures.

30. When operating an aircraft through Class D airspace or to an airport within Class D airspace, what requirement must be met? (14 CFR 91.129)

Each person must establish two-way radio communications with the ATC facilities providing air traffic services prior to entering that airspace and thereafter maintain those communications while within that airspace.

31. When departing a satellite airport without an operative control tower within Class D airspace, what requirement must be met? (14 CFR 91.129)

Each person must establish and maintain two-way radio communications with the ATC facility having jurisdiction over the Class D airspace area as soon as practicable after departing.

32. Is an ATC clearance required if flight operations are conducted through a Class D arrival extension area? (AIM 3-2-5, 3-2-6)

Arrival extensions for instrument approach procedures may be Class D or Class E airspace. Arrival extensions will either be charted as part of the basic surface area with the blue segmented line indicating Class D airspace or as a separate surface area indicated by the magenta segmented line (Class E airspace). Communications with air traffic control are required whenever you are in the Class D area.

33. What minimum weather conditions are required when conducting VFR flight operations within Class D airspace? (14 CFR 91.155)

VFR flight operations within Class D airspace require 3 statute miles flight visibility and cloud clearances of at least 500 feet below, 1,000 feet above and 2,000 feet horizontal to clouds.

34. How is Class D airspace depicted on navigational charts? (AIM 3-2-5)

Class D airspace areas are depicted on Sectional and Terminal charts with blue segmented lines, and on IFR Low Altitude charts with a boxed [D].

35. What type of Air Traffic Control services are provided when operating within Class D airspace? (AIM 3-2-5, 5-5-8, and 5-5-10)

No separation services are provided to VFR aircraft. When meteorological conditions permit, regardless of the type of flight plan or whether or not under the control of a radar facility, the pilot is responsible to see and avoid other traffic, terrain, or obstacles. A controller, on a workload permitting basis, will provide radar traffic information, safety alerts and traffic information for sequencing purposes.

36. What is the maximum speed an aircraft may be operated within Class D airspace? (14 CFR 91.117)

Unless otherwise authorized or required by ATC, no person may operate an aircraft at or below 2,500 feet above the surface within 4 nautical miles of the primary airport of a Class C or D airspace area at an indicated airspeed of more than 200 knots (230 mph).

37. What is the definition of Class E airspace? (AIM 3-2-6)

Generally, if the airspace is not Class A, Class B, Class C, or Class D, and it is controlled airspace, it is Class E airspace.

38. State several examples of Class E airspace. (AIM 3-2-6)

a. A surface area designated for an airport and configured to contain all instrument approaches.

b. An extension to a surface area—There are Class E airspace areas that serve as extensions to Class B, Class C, and Class D surface areas designated for an airport. Such airspace provides controlled airspace to contain standard instrument approach procedures.

c. Airspace used for transition—Class E airspace beginning at either 700 or 1,200 feet AGL used to transition to/from the terminal enroute environment.

d. En Route Domestic Areas—Class E airspace areas that extend upward from a specified altitude and provide controlled airspace in those areas where there is a requirement to provide IFR en route ATC services but the Federal airway system is inadequate.

e. Federal Airways—The Federal airways are Class E airspace
   areas, and unless otherwise specified, extend upward from
   1,200 feet AGL to, but not including 18,000 feet MSL.

f. Offshore Airspace areas—Class E airspace that extends upward
   from a specified altitude to, but not including 18,000 feet MSL.
   These areas provide controlled airspace beyond 12 miles from
   the coast of the United States in those areas where there is a
   requirement to provide IFR en route ATC services.

g. Unless designated at a lower altitude—Class E airspace begins
   at 14,500 feet MSL over the United States including that
   airspace overlying the waters within 12 nautical miles of the
   coast of the contiguous states and Alaska (excluding the Alaska
   peninsula west of 160°00'00"W) and the airspace less than
   1,500 feet above the surface of the earth.

39. What are the operating rules and pilot/equipment requirements to operate within Class E airspace? (AIM 3-2-6)

a. Minimum pilot certification—Student Pilot Certificate.

b. No specific equipment requirements in Class E airspace.

c. No specific requirements for arrival or through flight in
   Class E airspace.

40. What basic operational requirement must be met if flight operations are to be conducted into Class E surface area located at a non-tower airport with a prescribed instrument approach? (AIM 3-2-6)

As long as the weather allows flight operations to be conducted
under basic VFR minimums, a flight into or out of the Class E airspace may be made without an ATC clearance. However, if basic
VFR minimums cannot be maintained an ATC clearance will be
necessary for arrival or departure (Special VFR clearance).

41. How is Class E airspace depicted on navigational charts? (AIM 3-2-6)

Class E airspace below 14,500 feet MSL is charted on Sectional, Terminal, World, and IFR En Route Low Altitude charts. Class E airspace without an operating control tower but with prescribed instrument approaches is depicted with a magenta segmented line which denotes controlled airspace extending upward from the surface to the overlying floor of the adjacent controlled airspace. The vertical limit will not be depicted. Where the outer edge of the 700-foot Class E airspace (transition area, magenta shaded line) ends, the 1,200 foot or greater area automatically begins. (Blue shading for Class E airspace beginning at 1,200 feet is used only when it borders Class G airspace.)

42. What is the definition of Class G airspace? (AIM 3-3-1)

Class G airspace is that portion of the airspace that has not been designated as Class A, B, C, D and E airspace.

43. What is the minimum cloud clearance and visibility required when conducting flight operations in a traffic pattern at night in Class G airspace? (14 CFR 91.155)

When the visibility is less than 3 statute miles but not less than 1 statute mile during night hours, an airplane may be operated clear of clouds if operated in an airport traffic pattern within one-half mile of the runway.

44. What is the main difference between Class G and Class A, B, C, D, and E airspace?

The main difference that distinguishes Class G (uncontrolled) from Class A, B, C, D, E (controlled) airspace is the flight visibility/cloud clearance requirements necessary to operate within it.

45. What minimum flight visibility and clearance from clouds are required for VFR flight in the following situations? (14 CFR 91.155)

CLASS C, D, or E AIRSPACE (controlled airspace)
Less than 10,000 feet MSL:
Visibility: 3 statute miles.
Cloud clearance: 500 feet below, 1,000 feet above, 2,000 feet horizontal.

At or above 10,000 feet MSL:
Visibility: 5 statute miles.
Cloud clearance: 1,000 feet below, 1,000 feet above, 1 statute mile horizontal.

CLASS G AIRSPACE (uncontrolled airspace)
1,200 feet or less above the surface (regardless of MSL altitude):
DAY: Visibility: 1 statute mile.
Cloud clearance: clear of clouds.
NIGHT: Visibility: 3 statute miles.
Cloud clearance: 500 feet below, 1,000 feet above, 2,000 feet horizontal.

More than 1,200 feet above the surface but **less than** 10,000 feet MSL:
DAY: Visibility: 1 statute mile.
Cloud clearance: 500 feet below, 1,000 feet above, 2,000 feet horizontal.
NIGHT: Visibility: 3 statute miles.
Cloud clearance: 500 feet below, 1,000 feet above, 2,000 feet horizontal.

More than 1,200 feet above the surface and **at or above** 10,000 feet MSL:
Visibility: 5 statute miles.
Cloud clearance: 1,000 feet below, 1,000 feet above, 1 statute mile horizontal.

46. If VFR flight minimums cannot be maintained, can a VFR flight be made into Class B, C, D, or E airspace? (AIM 4-4-6)

No, with one exception. A "Special VFR clearance" may be obtained from the controlling authority prior to entering the Class B, C, D, or E airspace provided the flight can be made clear of clouds with at least one statute mile ground visibility if taking off or landing. If ground visibility is not reported at that airport, the flight visibility must be at least 1 statute mile.

47. Are Special VFR clearances always available to pilots in all classes of airspace? (AIM 4-4-6)

A VFR pilot may request and be given a clearance to enter, leave, or operate within most Class D and Class E surface areas and some Class B and Class C surface areas, traffic permitting, and providing such flight will not delay IFR operations.

Note: Special VFR operations by fixed-wing aircraft are prohibited in some Class B and Class C surface areas due to the volume of IFR traffic; a list of these areas is contained in 14 CFR Part 91 and also depicted on sectional aeronautical charts.

48. If it becomes apparent that a Special VFR clearance will be necessary, what facility should the pilot contact in order to obtain one? (AIM 4-4-6)

Within the Class B, C, or D surface area, requests for clearances should be to the tower. If no tower is located within the airspace (Class E airspace), a clearance may be obtained from the nearest tower, FSS, or center.

49. Can a "Special VFR clearance" be obtained into or out of Class B, C, D, or E airspace at night? (AIM 4-4-6)

Special VFR operations by fixed-wing aircraft are prohibited between sunset and sunrise unless the pilot is instrument rated and the aircraft is equipped for IFR flight.

50. Under what conditions, if any, may pilots enter restricted or prohibited areas? (14 CFR 91.133)

No person may operate an aircraft within a restricted area contrary to the restrictions imposed, or within a prohibited area, unless that person has the permission of the using or controlling agency.

Normally, *no* operations are permitted within a prohibited area and *prior* permission must always be obtained before operating within a restricted area.

51. What is a "TRSA"? (AIM 3-5-6)

A Terminal Radar Service Area (TRSA) consists of airspace surrounding designated airports wherein ATC provides radar vectoring, sequencing, and separation on a full-time basis for all IFR and participating VFR aircraft. Pilot participation is urged but not mandatory.

52. What class of airspace is a "TRSA"? (AIM 3-5-6)

TRSAs do not fit into any of the U.S. airspace classes and are not contained in 14 CFR Part 71 nor are there any operating rules in Part 91. The primary airport(s) within the TRSA become Class D airspace. The remaining portion of a TRSA overlies other controlled airspace which is normally Class E airspace beginning at 700 or 1,200 feet and established to transition to/from the en route/terminal environment. TRSAs will continue to be an airspace area where participating pilots can receive additional radar services which have been redefined as TRSA service.

53. How are TRSAs depicted on navigational charts? (AIM 3-5-6)

TRSAs are depicted on visual charts with a solid black line and altitudes for each segment. The Class D portion is charted with a blue segmented line.

54. What are TFRs? (FAA-H-8083-25)

Temporary Flight Restrictions are established to protect people and property in the air and on the ground from an existing or possible hazard. They can exist for a variety of reasons: the President or Vice President visiting an area, around disaster relief operations, in areas where NASA is conducting operations, and around nuclear plants.

55. How do you know if a TFR affects your planned flight? (FAA-H-8083-25)

They aren't depicted on a chart, pilots must check NOTAMs to find them. TFRs are no-fly-zones; pilots must get information about any TFRs along their route while on the ground and plan flights accordingly.

P. National Transportation Safety Board

1. When is immediate notification to the NTSB required? (NTSB 830)

The operator of an aircraft shall immediately, and by the most expeditious means available, notify the nearest NTSB field office when an aircraft accident or any of the following listed incidents occur:

- Failure of any internal turbine engine component that results in the escape of debris other than out the exhaust path.
- In-flight fire.
- Aircraft collision in flight.
- Release of all or a portion of a propeller blade from an aircraft, excluding release caused solely by ground contact.
- A complete loss of information, excluding flickering, from more than 50 percent of an aircraft's cockpit displays, including EFIS and PFD.
- Airborne Collision and Avoidance System (ACAS) resolution advisories issued either to an aircraft operating in Class A airspace, or when an aircraft is being operated on an IFR flight plan and compliance with the advisory is necessary to avoid a substantial risk of collision between two or more aircraft.
- Damage to helicopter tail or main rotor blades, including ground damage, that requires major repair or replacement of the blade(s).
- Any event in which an aircraft operated by an air carrier lands or departs on a taxiway, incorrect runway, or other area not designated as a runway, or experiences a runway incursion that requires the operator or the crew of another aircraft or vehicle to take immediate corrective action to avoid a collision.

Q. Airport Operations

1. What is the standard direction of turns when approaching an uncontrolled airport for landing? (AIM 4-3-4)

When approaching for landing, all turns must be made to the left unless a traffic pattern indicator indicates that turns should be made to the right.

2. What is considered standard for traffic pattern altitude? (AIM 4-3-3)

Unless otherwise established, 1,000 feet AGL is the recommended traffic pattern altitude. At most airports and military air bases, traffic pattern altitudes for propeller-driven aircraft generally extend from 600 feet to as high as 1,500 feet AGL. Also, traffic pattern altitudes for military turbojet aircraft sometimes extend up to 2,500 feet AGL.

3. When issued taxi instructions to an assigned takeoff runway, are you automatically authorized to cross any runway that intersects your taxi route? (AIM 4-3-18)

No; Aircraft must receive a runway crossing clearance for each runway that their taxi route crosses. When assigned a takeoff runway, ATC will first specify the runway, issue taxi instructions, and state any hold short instructions or runway crossing clearances if the taxi route will cross a runway. When issuing taxi instructions to any point other than an assigned takeoff runway, ATC will specify the point to taxi to, issue taxi instructions, and state any hold short instructions or runway crossing clearances if the taxi route will cross a runway. ATC is required to obtain a readback from the pilot of all runway hold short instructions.

4. Where are wake turbulence and wing-tip vortices likely to occur? (AIM 7-3-3)

All aircraft generate turbulence and associated wing-tip vortices. In general, avoid the area behind and below the generating aircraft, especially at low altitudes. Also of concern is the weight, speed, and shape of the wing of the generating aircraft. The greatest vortex strength occurs when the generating aircraft is HEAVY, CLEAN, and SLOW.

5. What operational procedures should be followed when wake vortices are suspected to exist? (AIM 7-3-6)

a. *Landing behind large aircraft on the same runway:* stay at or above the large aircraft's flight path. Note its touchdown point and land beyond it.

b. *Landing behind a departing large aircraft:* note the large aircraft's rotation point; land well prior to its rotation point.

c. *Departing behind a large aircraft on the same runway:* note the large aircraft's rotation point and rotate prior to its rotation point. Continue to climb above and upwind of its flight path.

d. *En route VFR:* avoid flight below and behind a large aircraft's path.

6. What is LAHSO? (AIM 4-3-11)

An acronym for "Land and Hold Short Operations." These include landing and holding short of an intersecting runway, an intersecting taxiway, or some other designated point on a runway. LAHSO is an ATC procedure that requires pilot participation to balance the needs for increased airport capacity and system efficiency.

7. When should you decline a LAHSO clearance?
(AIM 4-3-11)

Student pilots or pilots not familiar with LAHSO should not participate in the program. Pilots are expected to decline a LAHSO clearance if they determine it will compromise safety or if weather is below basic VFR weather conditions (a minimum ceiling of 1,000 feet and 3 SM visibility).

8. Where can available landing distance (ALD) data be found? (AIM 4-3-11)

ALD data is published in the special notices section of the A/FD and in the U.S. Terminal Procedures Publications. Controllers will also provide ALD data upon request.

9. What are the six types of signs installed at airports?
(AIM 2-3-9 through 2-3-13)

    a. *Mandatory instruction sign*—red background/white inscription; denotes an entrance to a runway, a critical area, or a prohibited area.

    b. *Location sign*—black background/yellow inscription/yellow border; do not have arrows; used to identify a taxiway or runway location, the boundary of the runway, or identify an ILS critical area.

    c. *Direction sign*—yellow background/black inscription; identifies the designation of the intersecting taxiway(s) leading out of an intersection that a pilot would expect to turn onto or hold short of.

    d. *Destination sign*—yellow background/black inscription and also contain arrows; provides information on locating runways, terminals, cargo areas, and civil aviation areas, etc.

    e. *Information sign*—yellow background/black inscription; used to provide the pilot with information on areas that can't be seen from the control tower, applicable radio frequencies, and noise abatement procedures, etc.

    f. *Runway distance remaining sign*—black background/white numeral inscription; indicates the distance of the remaining runway in thousands of feet.

10. What color are runway markings? Taxiway markings?
(AIM 2-3-2)

Markings for runways are white. Markings for taxiways, areas not intended for use by aircraft (closed and hazardous areas), and holding positions (even if they are on a runway) are yellow.

11. What airport marking aids will be used to indicate the following? (AIM 2-3-2 through 2-3-6)

Runway Threshold Markings—These come in two configurations. They either consist of eight longitudinal stripes of uniform dimensions disposed symmetrically about the runway centerline, or the number of stripes is related to the runway width. A threshold marking helps identify the beginning of the runway available for landing.

Displaced Threshold—A threshold located at a point on the runway other than the designated beginning of the runway. A displaced threshold reduces the length of runway available for landings. The portion of runway behind a displaced threshold is available for takeoffs in either direction. A ten-foot wide white threshold bar is located across the width of the runway at the displaced threshold. White arrows are located along the centerline in the area between the beginning of the runway and displaced threshold. White arrowheads are located across the width of the runway just prior to the threshold bar.

Runway Hold Position Markings—For taxiways, these markings indicate where an aircraft is supposed to stop when it does not have clearance to proceed onto the runway. They are also installed on runways only if the runway is normally used by air traffic control for "land, hold short" operations. They consist of four yellow lines, two solid and two dashed, spaced six inches apart and extending across the width of the taxiway or runway.

Temporarily closed runways and taxiways—Provides a visual indication to pilots that a runway/taxiway is temporarily closed. Yellow crosses are placed on the runway only at each end of the runway. Closed taxiways are blocked with barricades or may utilize a yellow cross at the entrance to the taxiway.

Permanently closed runways and taxiways—For runways and taxiways which are permanently closed, the lighting circuits will be disconnected. The runway threshold, runway designation, and touchdown markings are obliterated and yellow crosses are placed at each end of the runway and at 1,000-foot intervals.

R. Runway Incursion Avoidance

1. What are three major areas that contribute to runway incursions? (FAA-H-8083-3)

a. *Communications* — misunderstanding the given clearance; failure to communicate effectively

b. *Airport knowledge* — failure to navigate the airport correctly; unable to interpret airport signage

c. *Cockpit procedures for maintaining orientation* — failure to maintain situational awareness

2. Preflight planning for taxi operations should be an integral part of the pilot's flight planning process. What information should this include? (AC 91-73)

a. Review and understand airport signage, markings and lighting.

b. Review the airport diagram, planned taxi route, and identify any "hot spots."

c. Review the latest airfield NOTAMs and ATIS (if available) for taxiway/runway closures, construction activity, etc.

d. Conduct a pre-taxi/pre-landing briefing that includes the expected/assigned taxi route and any hold short lines and restrictions based on ATIS information or previous experience at the airport.

e. Plan for critical times and locations on the taxi route (complex intersections, crossing runways, etc.).

f. Plan to complete as many aircraft checklist items as possible prior to taxi.

3. What is an airport "hot spot"? (FAA-H-8261-1)

A "hot spot" is a runway safety-related problem area or intersection on an airport. Typically, hot spots are complex or confusing taxiway–taxiway or taxiway–runway intersections. A lack of visibility may exist at certain points and/or the tower may be unable to see those particular intersections. Pilots should be increasingly vigilant when approaching and taxiing through these intersections.

4. Why is use of "sterile cockpit" procedures important when conducting taxi operations? (AC 91-73)

Pilots must be able to focus on their duties without being distracted by non-flight-related matters unrelated to the safe and proper operation of the aircraft. Refraining from nonessential activities during ground operations is essential. Passengers should be briefed on the importance of minimizing conversations and questions during taxi as well as on arrival, from the time landing preparations begin until the aircraft is safely parked.

5. When should a pilot request "progressive" taxi instructions? (AIM 4-3-18)

If the pilot is unfamiliar with the airport or for any reason confusion exists as to the correct taxi routing, a request may be made for progressive taxi instructions, which include step-by-step routing directions.

6. After completing your pre-taxi/pre-landing briefing of the taxi route you "expect" to receive, ATC calls and gives you a different route. What potential pitfall is common in this situation? (AC 91-73)

A common pitfall of pre-taxi and pre-landing planning is setting expectations and then receiving different instructions from ATC. Pilots need to follow the instructions that they actually receive, and not the ones they expect to receive. Short term memory is of limited duration.

7. Why is it a good idea to write down taxi instructions, especially at larger or unfamiliar airports? (AC 91-73)

Writing down taxi instructions, especially complex instructions, can reduce a pilot's vulnerability to forgetting part of the instructions and provides a reference for read-back of instructions to ATC. It can also be used as a means of reconfirming the taxi route and any restrictions at any time during taxi operations.

8. **When issued taxi instructions to an assigned takeoff runway, are you automatically authorized to cross any runway that intersects your taxi route?** (AIM 4-3-18)

No; Aircraft must receive a runway crossing clearance for each runway that their taxi route crosses. When assigned a takeoff runway, ATC will first specify the runway, issue taxi instructions, and state any hold short instructions or runway crossing clearances if the taxi route will cross a runway. When issuing taxi instructions to any point other than an assigned takeoff runway, ATC will specify the point to which to taxi, issue taxi instructions, and state any hold short instructions or runway crossing clearances if the taxi route will cross a runway. ATC is required to obtain a read back from the pilot of all runway hold short instructions.

9. **When receiving taxi instructions from a controller, pilots should always read back what information?** (AIM 4-3-18)

a. The runway assignment.

b. Any clearance to enter a specific runway.

c. Any instruction to hold short of a specific runway or line up and wait.

10. **What are some recommended practices that can assist a pilot in maintaining situational awareness during taxi operations?** (AC 91-73)

a. A current airport diagram should be available for immediate reference during taxi.

b. Monitor ATC instructions/clearances issued to other aircraft for the "big picture."

c. Focus attention outside the cockpit while taxiing.

d. Use all available resources (airport diagrams, airport signs, markings, lighting, and ATC) to keep the aircraft on its assigned taxi route.

e. Cross-reference heading indicator to ensure turns are being made in the correct direction and that you're on the assigned taxi route.

f. Prior to crossing any hold short line, visually check for conflicting traffic; verbalize "clear left, clear right."

Continued

   g. Be alert for other aircraft with similar call signs on the
      frequency.

   h. Understand and follow all ATC instructions and if in
      doubt—Ask!

11. How can a pilot use aircraft exterior lighting to enhance situational awareness and safety during airport surface operations? (AC 91-73; SAFO)

To the extent possible and consistent with aircraft equipment, operating limitations, and pilot procedures, pilots should illuminate
exterior lights as follows:

   a. *Engines running*—Turn on the rotating beacon whenever an
      engine is running.

   b. *Taxiing*—Prior to commencing taxi, turn on navigation/position
      lights and anti-collision lights.

   c. *Crossing a runway*—All exterior lights should be illuminated
      when crossing a runway.

   d. *Entering the departure runway for takeoff*—All exterior lights
      (except landing lights) should be on to make your aircraft more
      conspicuous to aircraft on final and ATC.

   e. *Cleared for takeoff*—All exterior lights including takeoff/land-
      ing lights.

Note: If you see an aircraft in takeoff position on a runway with
landing lights ON, that aircraft has most likely received its takeoff
clearance and will be departing immediately.

12. During calm or nearly calm wind conditions, at an airport without an operating control tower, a pilot should be aware of what potentially hazardous situations? (AC 91-73)

Aircraft may be landing and/or taking off on more than one runway
at the airport. Also, aircraft may be using an instrument approach
procedure to runways other than the runway in use for VFR operations. The instrument approach runway may intersect the VFR runway. It is also possible that an instrument arrival may be made to
the opposite end of the runway from which a takeoff is being
made.

13. **You have just landed at a tower-controlled airport and missed your assigned taxiway for exiting the runway. Is it permissible for you to turn around on the runway and return to the exit taxiway?** (AIM 4-3-20)

No; At airports with an operating control tower, pilots should never stop or reverse course on the runway without first obtaining ATC approval.

14. **When taxiing at a non-towered airport, what are several precautionary measures you should take prior to entering or crossing a runway?** (AC 91-73)

Listen on the appropriate frequency (CTAF) for inbound aircraft information and always scan the full length of the runway, including the final approach and departure paths, before entering or crossing the runway. Self-announce your position and intentions and remember that not all aircraft are radio-equipped.

15. **ATC has instructed you to line up and wait on the departure runway due to crossing traffic on an intersecting taxiway. What is considered a reasonable amount of time to wait for a takeoff clearance before calling ATC?** (AIM 5-2-4; SAFO)

FAA analysis of accidents and incidents involving aircraft holding in position indicate that two minutes or more elapsed between the time the instruction was issued to line up and wait and the resulting event (for example, land-over or go-around). If you have been holding in position on the runway for more than 90 seconds, or you see or hear a potential conflict, contact ATC immediately.

16. **What is a Pilot Deviation?** (AC 61-98)

A pilot deviation (PD) is defined as an action of a pilot that results in the violation of a Federal aviation regulation. PDs are broadly classified as either airborne deviations or surface deviations. Within each of these two broad classifications are a number of sub-classifications. The principal areas of concern in the airborne classification include altitude deviations, course deviations, and airspace incursions. The principal area of concern within the surface deviation classification involves runway incursions, but surface deviations also include vehicle/pedestrian violations. While the outcomes of most PDs are benign, any deviation has the potential to be catastrophic. Because of this potential for catastrophic outcome, PDs are a major concern in both the aviation industry and within the FAA. For several years, PDs have been on the rise. Of particular concern is that a significant majority of all PDs (69%) are occurring during GA operations. The occurrence of incidents and PDs has emphasized the need to ensure that all pilots receive adequate briefing on PD avoidance awareness. Pilots should be familiar with all types of airspace, and ground operating procedures, and best practices to avoid potential PDs. The flight review may be the only regular proficiency and recurrency training experienced by some pilots. Therefore, CFIs should place appropriate emphasis on this part of the review.

S. Aviation Security

1. What are several actions you can take to enhance aircraft security? (TSA)

a. Always lock your aircraft.

b. Keep track of door/ignition keys and don't leave keys in unattended aircraft.

c. Use secondary locks (prop, tie down, throttle, and wheel locks) or aircraft disabler if available.

d. Lock hangar when unattended.

2. What type of airport security procedures should you review regularly to prevent unauthorized access to aircraft at your airport? (FSSAT)

a. Limitations on ramp access to people other than instructors and students

b. Standards for securing aircraft on the ramp

c. Securing access to aircraft keys at all times

d. New auxiliary security items for aircraft (prop locks, throttle locks, locking tie downs)

e. After-hours or weekend access procedures

3. Give some examples of what you would consider suspicious activity at an airport. (TSA)

a. Aircraft with unusual modifications (such as modified N-numbers) or activity

b. Unfamiliar persons loitering for extended periods in the vicinity of parked aircraft

c. Anyone making threats

d. Events or circumstances that do not fit the pattern of lawful, normal activity at an airport

e. Pilots appearing to be under the control of others

4. When witnessing suspicious or criminal activity, what are three basic ways for reporting the suspected activity? (TSA)

If you determine that it's safe, question the individual. If their response is unsatisfactory and they continue to act suspiciously:

a. Alert airport or FBO management.

b. Contact local law enforcement if the activity poses an immediate threat to persons or property.

c. Contact the 866-GA-SECURE hotline to document the reported event.

5. What is the purpose of the 866-GA-SECURE phone number? (TSA)

866-GA-SECURE is a toll-free hotline operated by the Transportation Security Administration (TSA) Security Operations Center. It is staffed 24/7 to take reports of suspicious or criminal activity occurring at general aviation airports. TSA personnel will document the reported activity, collect your personal contact numbers, and pass the information on to the appropriate regulatory office within the TSA.

Note: Calling 866-GA-SECURE will not dispatch local law enforcement. In the event of an immediate emergency, 911 or local law enforcement should be contacted first.

6. **What are several sources of information available to pilots interested in additional guidance on aviation security?** (TSA; FSSAT)

Security Guidelines for General Aviation Airports is a set of federally endorsed guidelines that offers an extensive list of options, ideas, and suggestions for the airport operator, sponsor, tenant and/or user to choose from when considering security enhancements for GA facilities.

Flight School Security Awareness Training for Aircraft and Simulators is an online training course designed to raise the general security awareness levels of employees working in the flight training industry.

T. Aircraft and Engine Operations

1. **What type of fuel does your aircraft require (minimum octane rating and color)?**

The approved fuel grade used is 100LL and the color is blue (for most airplanes).

2. **Can other types of fuel be used if the specified grade is not available?** (FAA-H-8083-25)

You may use fuel of a higher grade but only as a temporary solution. You should never use a fuel of a lower grade such as 80/87. If you must use a different grade of fuel, use a grade as close as possible to 100LL such as 100/130 or 115/145, and use it only for a short period of time. Always reference the aircraft's AFM or POH.

U. System and Equipment Malfunctions

1. What causes "carburetor icing" and what are the first indications of its presence? (FAA-H-8083-25)

The vaporization of fuel, combined with the expansion of air as it passes through the carburetor, causes a sudden cooling of the mixture. The temperature of the air passing through the carburetor may drop as much as 60°F within a fraction of a second. Water vapor is squeezed out by this cooling, and if the temperature in the carburetor reaches 32°F or below, the moisture will be deposited as frost or ice inside the carburetor. For airplanes with a fixed-pitch propeller, the first indication of carburetor icing is loss of rpm. For airplanes with controllable-pitch (constant-speed) propellers, the first indication is usually a drop in manifold pressure.

2. What action should be taken if detonation is suspected? (FAA-H-8083-25)

Corrective action for detonation may be accomplished by adjusting any of the engine controls which will reduce both temperature and pressure of the fuel air charge.

a. Reduce power.

b. Reduce the climb rate for better cooling.

c. Enrich the fuel/air mixture.

d. Open cowl flaps if available.

Also, ensure that the airplane has been serviced with the proper grade of fuel.

3. What actions should be taken if preignition is suspected? (FAA-H-8083-25)

Corrective actions for preignition include any type of engine operation which would promote cooling such as:

a. Enrich the fuel/air mixture.

b. Reduce power.

c. Reduce the climb rate for better cooling.

d. Open cowl flaps if available.

4. Interpret the following ammeter indications.

a. Ammeter indicates a right deflection (positive).

- *After starting*—Power from the battery used for starting is being replenished by the alternator; or, if a full-scale charge is indicated for more than 1 minute, the starter is still engaged and a shutdown is indicated.

- *During flight*—A faulty voltage regulator is causing the alternator to overcharge the battery. Reset the system and if the condition continues, terminate the flight as soon as possible.

b. Ammeter indicates a left deflection (negative).

- *After starting*—It is normal during start. At other times this indicates the alternator is not functioning or an overload condition exists in the system. The battery is not receiving a charge.

- *During flight*—The alternator is not functioning or an overload exists in the system. The battery is not receiving a charge. Possible causes: the master switch was accidentally shut off, or the alternator circuit breaker tripped.

5. What action should be taken if the ammeter indicates a continuous discharge while in flight?

The alternator has quit producing a charge, so the alternator circuit breaker should be checked and reset if necessary. If this does not correct the problem, the following should be accomplished:

a. The alternator should be turned off; pull the circuit breaker (the field circuit will continue to draw power from the battery).

b. All electrical equipment not essential to flight should be turned off (the battery is now the only source of electrical power).

6. What action should be taken if the ammeter indicates a continuous charge while in flight (more than two needle widths)?

If a continuous excessive rate of charge were allowed for any extended period of time, the battery would overheat and evaporate the electrolyte at an excessive rate. A possible explosion of the battery could result. Also, electronic components in the electrical system would be adversely affected by higher than normal voltage. Protection is provided by an overvoltage sensor which will shut the alternator down if an excessive voltage is detected. If this should occur, the following should be done:

a. The alternator should be turned off; pull the circuit breaker (the field circuit will continue to draw power from the battery).

b. All electrical equipment not essential to flight should be turned off (the battery is now the only source of electrical power).

c. The flight should be terminated and a landing made as soon as possible.

7. During a cross-country flight you notice that the oil pressure is low, but the oil temperature is normal. What is the problem and what action should be taken?

A low oil pressure in flight could be the result of any one of several problems, the most common being that of insufficient oil. If the oil temperature continues to remain normal, a clogged oil pressure relief valve or an oil pressure gauge malfunction could be the culprit. In any case, a landing at the nearest airport is advisable to check for the cause of trouble.

8. What procedures should be followed concerning a partial loss of power in flight?

If a partial loss of power occurs, the first priority is to establish and maintain a suitable airspeed (best glide airspeed if necessary). Then, select an emergency landing area and remain within gliding distance. As time allows, attempt to determine the cause and correct it. Complete the following checklist:

a. Check the carburetor heat.

b. Check the amount of fuel in each tank and switch fuel tanks if necessary.

c. Check the fuel selector valve's current position.

d. Check the mixture control.

e. Check that the primer control is all the way in and locked.

f. Check the operation of the magnetos in all three positions; both, left or right.

9. What procedures should be followed if an engine fire develops on the ground during starting?

Continue to attempt an engine start as a start will cause flames and excess fuel to be sucked back through the carburetor.

a. If the engine starts:
   • Increase the power to a higher RPM for a few moments; and
   • shut down the engine and inspect it.

b. If the engine does not start:
   • Set the throttle to the "Full" position.
   • Set the mixture control to "Idle cutoff."
   • Continue to try an engine start in an attempt to put out the fire by vacuum.

c. If the fire continues:
   • Turn the ignition switch to "Off."
   • Turn the master switch to "Off."
   • Set the fuel selector to "Off."

In all cases, evacuate the aircraft and obtain a fire extinguisher and/or fire personnel assistance.

10. What procedures should be followed if an engine fire develops in flight?

In the event of an engine fire in flight, the following procedures should be used:

a. Set the mixture control to "Idle cutoff."

b. Set the fuel selector valve to "Off."

c. Turn the master switch to "Off."

d. Set the cabin heat and air vents to "Off"; leave the overhead vents "On."

e. Establish an airspeed of 100 KIAS and increase the descent, if necessary, to find an airspeed that will provide for an incombustible mixture.

f. Execute a forced landing procedures checklist.

V. Airplane Instruments

1. What are the various compass errors? (FAA-H-8083-15)

Oscillation error — Erratic movement of the compass card caused by turbulence or rough control technique.

Deviation error — Due to electrical and magnetic disturbances in the aircraft.

Variation error — Angular difference between true and magnetic north; reference isogonic lines of variation.

Dip errors:

> *Acceleration error* — On east or west headings, while accelerating, the magnetic compass shows a turn to the north, and when decelerating, it shows a turn to the south.
>
> *Remember:* ANDS
>
> **A** ccelerate
> **N** orth
> **D** ecelerate
> **S** outh
>
> *Northerly turning error* — The compass leads in the south half of a turn, and lags in the north half of a turn.
>
> *Remember:* UNOS
>
> **U** ndershoot
> **N** orth
> **O** vershoot
> **S** outh

W. Aeromedical Factors

1. What factors can make a pilot more susceptible to hypoxia? (AIM 8-1-2)

The altitude at which significant effects of hypoxia occur can be lowered by a number of factors. Carbon monoxide inhaled in smoking or from exhaust fumes, lowered hemoglobin (anemia), and certain medications can reduce the oxygen-carrying capacity of the blood. Small amounts of alcohol and low doses of certain drugs, such as antihistamines, tranquilizers, sedatives, and analgesics can, through their depressant action, render the brain much more susceptible to hypoxia. Extreme heat and cold, fever, and anxiety increase the body's demand for oxygen, and hence its susceptibility to hypoxia.

2. What symptoms can a pilot expect from hyperventilation? (AIM 8-1-3)

As hyperventilation "blows off" excessive carbon dioxide from the body, a pilot can experience symptoms of lightheadedness, suffocation, drowsiness, tingling in the extremities, and coolness, and react to them with even greater hyperventilation. Incapacitation can eventually result from uncoordination, disorientation, and painful muscle spasms. Finally, unconsciousness can occur.

3. How does carbon monoxide poisoning occur and for what symptoms should a pilot be alert? (AIM 8-1-4)

Most heaters in light aircraft work by air flowing over the manifold. The use of these heaters while exhaust fumes are escaping through manifold cracks and seals is responsible every year for several nonfatal and fatal aircraft accidents from carbon monoxide poisoning. A pilot who detects the odor of exhaust or experiences symptoms of headache, drowsiness, or dizziness while using the heater should suspect carbon monoxide poisoning.

4. What regulations apply and what common sense should prevail concerning the use of alcohol? (14 CFR 91.17)

The regulations prohibit pilots from performing crewmember duties within 8 hours after drinking any alcoholic beverage, while under the influence of alcohol, or having .04 percent weight or more alcohol in the blood. Due to the slow destruction of alcohol in the bloodstream, a pilot may still be under the influence, or over the .04 percent mark, 8 hours after drinking a moderate amount of alcohol. Therefore, an excellent rule is to allow at least 12 to 24 hours from "bottle to throttle," depending on the amount of alcoholic beverage consumed.

5. What regulations apply and what common sense should prevail concerning the use of drugs and medication? (14 CFR 91.17)

Pilot performance can be seriously degraded by both prescribed and over-the-counter medications, as well as by the medical conditions for which they are taken. The regulations prohibit pilots from performing crewmember duties while using any medication that affects the faculties in any way contrary to safety. The safest rule is not to fly as a crewmember while taking any medication, unless approved to do so by the FAA.

6. What method does the FAA encourage pilots to use as a logical way to approach decision making? (AC 60-22)

The DECIDE Model is a six-step, continuous-loop decision-making process which can be used to assist a pilot when he/she is faced with a situation requiring judgment:

Detect—the decisionmaker detects the fact that change has occurred.

Estimate—the decisionmaker estimates the need to counter or react to the change.

Choose—the decisionmaker chooses a desirable outcome (in terms of success for the flight).

Identify—the decisionmaker identifies actions that could successfully control the change.

Do—the decisionmaker takes the necessary action.

Evaluate—the decisionmaker evaluates the effect(s) of his/her action countering the change.

7. What are the 5 types of hazardous attitudes the FAA has identified and provided antidotes for, to encourage pilots to develop a realistic perspective on attitudes toward flying? (AC 60-22)

Antiauthority (Don't tell me!) — Follow the rules, they are usually right.

Impulsivity (Do something quickly!)—Not so fast. Think first.

Invulnerability (It won't happen to me.)—It could happen to me.

Macho (I can do it)—Taking chances is foolish.

Resignation (What's the use?)— I'm not helpless, I can make a difference.

X. Single-Pilot Resource Management

1. Define the term "risk management." (FAA-H-8083-9)

Risk management is a decision-making process designed to systematically identify hazards, assess the degree of risk, and determine the best course of action. It is a logical process of weighing the potential costs of risks against the possible benefits of allowing those risks to stand uncontrolled.

2. How can the use of the "PAVE" checklist during flight planning help you to assess risk? (FAA-H-8083-9)

Use of the PAVE checklist provides pilots with a simple way to remember each category to examine for risk during flight planning. The pilot divides the risks of flight into four categories:

Pilot-In-Command—general health, physical/mental/emotional state, proficiency, currency

Aircraft—airworthiness, equipment, performance capability

enVironment—weather hazards, terrain, airports/runways to be used, conditions

External pressures—meetings, people waiting at destination, desire to impress someone, etc.

3. Explain the use of a "personal minimums" checklist and how it can help a pilot control risk. (FAA-H-8083-9)

One of the most important concepts that safe pilots understand is the difference between what is "legal" in terms of the regulations, and what is "smart" or "safe" in terms of pilot experience and proficiency. One way a pilot can control the risks is to set personal minimums for items in each risk category. These are limits unique to that individual pilot's current level of experience and proficiency.

4. Explain the use of a personal checklist such as "I'M SAFE" to determine personal risks. (FAA-H-8083-9)

Personal, self-assessment checklists assist pilots in conducting pre-flight checks on themselves, reviewing their physical and emotional states that could have an effect on their performance. The "I'M SAFE" checklist reminds pilots to consider the following:

Illness—Do I have any symptoms?

Medication—Have I been taking prescription or over-the-counter drugs?

Stress—Am I under psychological pressure from my job? Do I have money, family or health problems?

Alcohol—Have I been drinking within 8 hours? Within 24 hours?

Fatigue—Am I tired and not adequately rested?

Eating—Am I adequately nourished?

5. Define the term "task management." (FAA-H-8083-9)

Task management is the process by which pilots manage the many, concurrent tasks that must be performed to safely and efficiently operate an aircraft.

6. What are the different tasks that task management may consist of at any given time? (FAA-H-8083-9)

a. *Initiation* of new tasks

b. *Monitoring* of ongoing tasks to determine their status

c. *Prioritization* of tasks based on importance, status, urgency, and other factors

d. *Allocation* of human and machine resources to high-priority tasks

e. *Interruption* and subsequent resumption of lower priority tasks

f. *Termination* of tasks that have been completed or are no longer relevant

7. **What are several options that a pilot can employ to decrease workload and avoid becoming overloaded?** (FAA-H-8083-25)

Stop, think, slow down, and prioritize. Tasks such as locating an item on a chart or setting a radio frequency may be delegated to another pilot or passenger; an autopilot, if available, may be used; or ATC may be enlisted to provide assistance.

8. **What is one method of prioritizing tasks to avoid an overload situation?** (FAA-H-8083-25)

During any situation, and especially in an emergency, remember the phrase "aviate, navigate, and communicate."

9. **How can tasks be completed in a timely manner without causing a distraction from flying?** (FAA-H-8083-9)

By planning, prioritizing, and sequencing tasks, a potential work overload situation can be avoided. As experience is gained, a pilot learns to recognize future workload requirements and can prepare for high workload periods during times of low workload.

10. **Why are pilots encouraged to use checklists?** (FAA-H-8083-3)

The checklist is an aid to the memory and helps to ensure that critical items necessary for the safe operation of aircraft are not overlooked or forgotten. They provide a standardized method for verifying aircraft configuration and a logical sequence for accomplishing tasks inside and outside the cockpit.

11. **What are two common methods of checklist usage?** (Order 8900.1)

a. *Do-Verify (DV) method*—consists of the checklist being accomplished in a variable sequence without a preliminary challenge. After all of the action items on the checklist have been completed, the checklist is then read again while each item is verified. The DV method allows the pilot/flightcrew to use flow patterns from memory to accomplish a series of actions quickly and efficiently.

b. *Challenge-Do-Verify (CDV) method*—consists of a pilot/crew-member making a challenge before an action is initiated, taking the action, and then verifying that the action item has been accomplished. The CDV method is most effective in two-pilot crews where one crewmember issues the challenge and the second crewmember takes the action and responds to the first crewmember, verifying that the action was taken.

12. What are several examples of common errors that can occur when using a checklist?

a. Checklist items are missed because of distraction or interruption (by passengers, ATC, etc.).

b. Checklist items are incorrectly performed (hurrying checklist; reading item but not verifying or setting).

c. Failure to use the appropriate checklist for a specific phase of flight.

d. Too much time spent with head down, reading the checklist and compromising safety.

e. Checklist is not readily accessible in cockpit.

f. Emergency/abnormal procedures checklist is not readily available.

g. Memory items accomplished but not confirmed with checklist.

13. In what phases of flight should a prepared checklist be used? (FAA-H-8083-3)

a. Preflight inspection

b. Before engine start

c. Engine starting

d. Before taxiing

e. Before takeoff

f. After takeoff

g. Cruise

h. Descent

i. Before landing

j. After landing

k. Engine shutdown and securing

14. What are several recommended methods for managing checklist accomplishment? (Order 8900.1)

a. The pilot should touch/point at each control, display or switch.

b. Verbally state the desired status of the checklist item.

c. When complete, announce that "___ checklist is complete."

15. What are "immediate action" items? (Order 8900.1)

An immediate action item is an action that must be accomplished so expeditiously (in order to avoid or stabilize a hazardous situation) that time is not available for the pilot/crewmember to refer to a manual or checklist. Once the emergency has been brought under control, the pilot refers to the actual checklist to verify that all immediate action items were accomplished. Only after this is done should the remainder of the checklist be completed.

16. Define the term "situational awareness." (FAA-H-8083-25)

Situational awareness (SA) is the accurate perception and understanding of all the factors and conditions within the four fundamental risk elements (pilot, aircraft, environment, external pressures) that affect safety before, during, and after the flight.

17. What are some of the elements inside and outside the aircraft that a pilot must consider to maintain situational awareness? (FAA-H-8083-9)

Inside the aircraft—the status of aircraft systems, pilot, and passengers

Outside the aircraft—awareness of where the aircraft is in relation to terrain, traffic, weather, and airspace

18. What are several factors that reduce situational awareness? (FAA-H-8083-15)

Factors that reduce SA include fatigue, distractions, unusual or unexpected events, complacency, high workload, unfamiliar situations, and inoperative equipment.

19. **When flying a technically advanced aircraft (TAA), what are several procedures that help ensure that situational awareness is enhanced, not diminished, by the automation?** (FAA-H-8083-25)

    Two basic procedures are to always double-check the system and to use verbal callouts. At a minimum, ensure the presentation makes sense. Was the correct destination fed into the navigation system? Callouts, even for single-pilot operations, are an excellent way to maintain situational awareness as well as manage information.

20. **What additional procedures can be used for maintaining situational awareness in technically advanced aircraft?** (FAA-H-8083-25)

    a. Perform verification checks of all programming prior to departure.

    b. Check the flight routing—ensure all routing matches the planned route of flight.

    c. Always verify waypoints.

    d. Make use of all onboard navigation equipment—use VOR to backup GPS, and vice versa.

    e. Match the use of the automated system with pilot proficiency—stay within personal limitations.

    f. Plan a realistic flight route to maintain situational awareness—ATC doesn't always give you direct routing.

    g. Be ready to verify computer data entries—incorrect keystrokes can lead to loss of situational awareness.

21. **A majority of controlled flight into terrain (CFIT) accidents have been attributed to what factors?** (AC 61-134)

    a. Lack of pilot currency

    b. Loss of situational awareness

    c. Pilot distractions and breakdown of SRM

    d. Failure to comply with minimum safe altitudes

    e. Breakdown in effective ADM

    f. Insufficient planning, especially for the descent and arrival segments

22. A pilot can decrease the likelihood of a CFIT accident at the destination by identifying what risk factors prior to flight? (FAA-H-8261-1)

Factors such as airport location, runway lighting, weather/daylight conditions, approach specifications, ATC capabilities and limitations, type of operation, departure procedures, controller/pilot phraseology, and crew configuration should all be considered prior to flight.

23. Describe several operational techniques that will help you avoid a CFIT accident. (AC 61-134)

a. Maintain situational awareness at all times.

b. Adhere to safe takeoff and departure procedures.

c. Familiarize yourself with surrounding terrain features and obstacles.

d. Adhere to published routes and minimum altitudes.

e. Fly a stabilized approach.

f. Understand ATC clearances and instructions.

g. Don't become complacent.

24. What does the term "automation management" refer to? (FAA-H-8083-9)

Automation management is the demonstrated ability to control and navigate an aircraft by means of the automated systems installed in the aircraft. It includes understanding whether and when to use automated systems, including, but not limited to, the GPS and the autopilot.

25. In what three areas must a pilot be proficient when using advanced avionics or any automated system? (FAA-H-8083-25)

The pilot must know what to expect, how to monitor the system for proper operation, and be prepared to promptly take appropriate action if the system does not perform as expected.

26. What is the most important aspect of managing an autopilot/FMS? (FAA-H-8083-9)

Knowing at all times which modes are engaged, which modes are armed to engage, and being capable of verifying that armed functions (e.g. navigation tracking or altitude capture) engage at the appropriate time.

27. At a minimum, the pilot flying with advanced avionics must know how to manage what three primary items? (FAA-H-8083-25)

The course deviation indicator (CDI), the navigation source, and the autopilot.

28. Automation management is a good place to practice the standard callout technique. What are standard callouts? (FAA-H-8261-1)

To assist in maintaining situational awareness, professional flight crews often use standard callouts. For example, the non-flying pilot may call 2,000 and 1,000 feet prior to reaching an assigned altitude. The callout may be, "two to go" and "one to go." Single pilot operations can also benefit from this practice by adopting standard set callouts that can be used in the different segments of a flight. Examples of standard callouts are: "Power Set", "Airspeed Alive", "Rotate", "Positive Rate—Gear Up", "Localizer Alive", "Glideslope Alive", "Nav Source Verified", "Approach Mode Armed", "Approach Mode Active", "Final Approach Fix", etc.

Review: Sample Written Exercise

Candidate Information

Name:

_____

Certificate:

_____

Ratings:

_____

Flight review expiration date: _____

Class of Medical: _____

Medical expiration date: _____

1. A flight review must contain: _____ ground training _____ flight training.

2. The ground portion of the flight review must contain a comprehensive review of Part _____ .

3. The flight portion of the flight review must contain those maneuvers _____ .

4. What flights must be logged in a logbook? _____
   _____

5. In order to carry passengers, you must have made _____ landings in the category and class within the previous _____ days.

6. What information must a pilot familiarize him/herself with before each flight?_____
   _____

7. No person may pilot an aircraft within _____ hours of consumption of any alcoholic beverage.

8. What drugs cannot be taken before a flight?_____
   _____

9. A parachute is necessary if a pilot is carrying a passenger, if a bank angle of _____ degrees or a nose up or down angle of _____ degrees for any intentional maneuver is exceeded.

10. Fuel reserves for VFR flight are: day _____ night _____ .

11. Where is a transponder (with Mode C) necessary?

    a. _____

    b. _____

    c. _____

    d. _____

    e. _____

12. Oxygen is required above _____ feet regardless of the time flown at that altitude.

13. What three flight instruments are required for this flight?

    a. _____

    b. _____

    c. _____

14. An ELT is required if a training flight goes beyond _____ miles from your departure point and the aircraft is equipped to carry more than one person.

15. When aircraft are approaching head on, each aircraft shall alter their course to the _____ .

16. No person may perform aerobatics below _____ feet.

17. The minimum altitude over a congested area is _____ feet above the highest obstacle within _____ feet horizontally.

18. Two-way radio communications are necessary within Class(es)_____ airspace.

19. The standard pattern at an airport without a control tower and no visual pattern markings is _____-hand turns.

20. Clearance from ATC is necessary to penetrate Class(es) _____ airspace.

21. You may not operate in _____ or _____ areas without permission of the controlling agency.

22. You may not operate in Class A airspace under _____ flight rules.

23. Basic VFR weather minimums in controlled airspace below 10,000 feet are _____ miles visibility and _____ below, _____ above, and _____ horizontally from clouds.

24. VFR minimums in Class G airspace, under 10,000 feet, daytime, are _____ mile(s) visibility and _____ of clouds.

25. Under Special VFR, daytime, you may operate with visibility at least _____ miles and _____ of clouds when cleared by ATC.

26. When is an instrument rating required to operate under Special VFR?_____

27. When operating below 18,000 feet MSL and above 3,000 AGL, you should cruise at _____ thousands plus 500 feet on a mag course of 360 through 179 degrees, and _____ thousands plus 500 feet on a mag course of 180 through 359 degrees.

28. The maximum allowable gross weight for this aircraft is _____ pounds.

29. Our takeoff gross weight is _____ pounds.

30. Our center of gravity is _____ and is within limits (show work).

31. Our fuel minimum for this flight is _____ gallons.

32. Our stall speed in a clean configuration is _____ mph/kts (circle one).

33. You cannot spin the airplane if you keep the nose _____ the horizon and keep the ball _____ .

34. Spin recovery for this airplane requires: _____ _____ .

35. You must always enter the traffic pattern at a 45 degree angle to the downwind. True / False

36. The traffic pattern for this flight should be at _____ feet MSL, and _____ feet AGL.

37. The most important thing to do in the event of engine failure is to maintain _____ speed.

38. What is the meaning of each light signal?

Signal	Air	Ground
Steady Green		
Flashing Green		
Steady Red		
Flashing Red		
Flashing White		
Alternating Red & Green		

3 Ground Instruction Requirement

Flight Instruction Requirement

4

4 Flight Instruction Requirement

Maneuvers Tables

Although the flight review is *not* a checkride, a review of the practical test standards can offer some review into the standards your certificate is based on. These tolerances are not mandatory for a successful flight review, but they do demonstrate safe and skillful flying.

Private Pilot Practical Test Standards (condensed)

Task	Objective Minimum acceptable standard of performance			
Takeoff Normal/Crosswind Short/Soft	V_Y +10 / -5 V_X +10 / -5, then V_Y +10 / -5			
Landing Normal/Crosswind Forward Slip Short Soft Go Around	1.3 V_{S0} +10 / -5, touch at or within 400 feet beyond target Min float, touch at or within 400 feet beyond target 1.3 V_{S0} +10 / -5, touch at or within 200 feet beyond target 1.3 V_{S0} +10 / -5, touch at minimum speed and descent rate Power (Carb Heat off?), pitch for V_Y +10 / -5, flaps, gear			
Emergency Operations Emergency Approach and Landing	Use recommended descent configuration and airspeed ±10 kts.			
		Heading or bank ±°	**Altitude ± ft**	**Speed ± kts**
Traffic Pattern	Accurate track and safe spacing		100	10
Pilotage/NAV/Diverting	Know position ± 3 NM	15	200	ETA ±5min
Instrument Flying Straight and level Constant airspeed climb and descend Turns and rollouts on heading Communications, Navigation, Radar Services Recovery from unusual attitudes	 Recover to stabilized flight w/o excesses	20 20 10 20	200 200 200 200	10 10 10 10
Slow Flight and Stalls (no flight below 1,500 AGL) Power-off Stalls Power-on Stalls Maneuvering during Slow Flight Straight & level, turns, climbs, descents	 S & L or max. 20° bank Full-stall then recover S & L or max. 20° bank Full-stall then recover	 10 10 10	 100	 MCA+10/-0
Performance Maneuvers Steep turns 360° with 45° ±5° bank, coordinated		10	100	10
Ground Reference Maneuvers	Remain 600–1,000 AGL		100	10

Commerical Pilot Practical Test Standards (condensed)

Task	Objective Minimum acceptable standard of performance			
Takeoff Normal/Crosswind Soft Short	V_Y ±5 V_X (or mfr's recommended) ±5, then V_Y ±5 V_X (or 1.3 V_{S0}) ±5, -0 then V_Y ±5			
Landing Normal Short Soft Go Around	±5 of mfr, touch at or within 200 feet beyond target ±5 of mfr, touch at or within 100 feet beyond target ±5 of mfr V_Y ±5 after power pitch for initial mfr speed, flaps, gear			
Power-off 180° Accuracy Approach & Landing	1,000 feet AGL abeam touchdown point on downwind, power off, touch at or within 200 feet beyond target			
		Heading or bank ±°	**Altitude ± ft**	**Speed ± kts**
Traffic Pattern	Accurate track and safe spacing		100	10
Slow Flight & Maximum Performance (no flight below 1,500 AGL)				
STALLS Power on Power off Accelerated	S&L ±5°, max bank 20° S&L ±10°, max bank 20° Steady flight, below V_A, 20 kts above unaccel. stall speed	10° bank in turn 5° bank in turn apx 45° bank		
SLOW FLIGHT V_{MCA} Straight & level, turns, climbs, descents		5° bank angle 10° heading	50	MCA +5/-0
STEEP TURN 360° with 50° bank, ±5° coordinated		5° bank 10° heading	100	10
STEEP SPIRAL 360° descending turn	60° bank	10° Hdg on rollout	100	10
CHANDELLE Coordinated, positive control		10° Hdg @ 180	50	V_{MCA} on rollout
LAZY EIGHTS Coordinated, positive control, orientation		10° Hdg @ 180	100	10
Ground Reference Maneuvers EIGHTS ON PYLONS	S&L b/w pylons line of sight reference line on pylon, bank 30–40°			
Emergency Approach	Maintain mfr. glide ±10 kts while using checklist en route best site			

Excerpt from Federal Aviation Regulations

Appendix 1

1 Appendix

Excerpt: 14 CFR Part 61

§61.56 Flight review.

(a) Except as provided in paragraphs (b) and (f) of this section, a flight review consists of a minimum of 1 hour of flight training and 1 hour of ground training. The review must include:

    (1) A review of the current general operating and flight rules of part 91 of this chapter; and

    (2) A review of those maneuvers and procedures that, at the discretion of the person giving the review, are necessary for the pilot to demonstrate the safe exercise of the privileges of the pilot certificate.

(b) Glider pilots may substitute a minimum of three instructional flights in a glider, each of which includes a flight to traffic pattern altitude, in lieu of the 1 hour of flight training required in paragraph (a) of this section.

(c) Except as provided in paragraphs (d), (e), and (g) of this section, no person may act as pilot in command of an aircraft unless, since the beginning of the 24th calendar month before the month in which that pilot acts as pilot in command, that person has—

    (1) Accomplished a flight review given in an aircraft for which that pilot is rated by an authorized instructor; and

    (2) A logbook endorsed from an authorized instructor who gave the review certifying that the person has satisfactorily completed the review.

(d) A person who has, within the period specified in paragraph (c) of this section, passed a pilot proficiency check conducted by an examiner, an approved pilot check airman, or a U.S. Armed Force, for a pilot certificate, rating, or operating privilege need not accomplish the flight review required by this section.

(e) A person who has, within the period specified in paragraph (c) of this section, satisfactorily accomplished one or more phases of an FAA-sponsored pilot proficiency award program need not accomplish the flight review required by this section.

Continued

(f) A person who holds a flight instructor certificate and who has, within the period specified in paragraph (c) of this section, satisfactorily completed a renewal of a flight instructor certificate under the provisions in §61.197 need not accomplish the one hour of ground training specified in paragraph (a) of this section.

(g) A student pilot need not accomplish the flight review required by this section provided the student pilot is undergoing training for a certificate and has a current solo flight endorsement as required under §61.87 of this part.

(h) The requirements of this section may be accomplished in combination with the requirements of §61.57 and other applicable recent experience requirements at the discretion of the authorized instructor conducting the flight review.

(i) A flight simulator or flight training device may be used to meet the flight review requirements of this section subject to the following conditions:

(1) The flight simulator or flight training device must be used in accordance with an approved course conducted by a training center certificated under part 142 of this chapter.

(2) Unless the flight review is undertaken in a flight simulator that is approved for landings, the applicant must meet the takeoff and landing requirements of §61.57(a) or §61.57(b) of this part.

(3) The flight simulator or flight training device used must represent an aircraft or set of aircraft for which the pilot is rated.

[Docket No. 25910, 62 FR 16298, April 4, 1997; as amended by Amdt. 61–103, 62 FR 40898, July 30, 1997; Amdt. 61–104, 63 FR 20287, April 23, 1998; Amdt. 61–124, 74 FR 42550, Aug. 21, 2009]

Advisory Circular: AC 61-98B Excerpt

Appendix 2

Advisory Circular

Subject: **Currency Requirements and Guidance for the Flight Review and Instrument Proficiency Check**

Date: 4/30/12

Initiated by: AFS-800

AC No: **61-98B**

CHAPTER 1. GENERAL

1-1. PURPOSE. This advisory circular (AC) provides information for certificated pilots and flight instructors to use in complying with the flight review required by Title 14 of the Code of Federal Regulations (14 CFR) part 61, § 61.56 and the recent flight experience requirements of § 61.57.

1-2. CANCELLATION. This AC cancels AC 61-98A, Currency and Additional Qualification Requirements for Certificated Pilots, current edition. You can now find information on transition training in the current edition of FAA-H-8083-3, Airplane Flying Handbook.

1-3. RELATED CFR SECTIONS:

- Section 61.189, Flight instructor records.
- Section 61.193, Flight instructor privileges.
- Section 61.195, Flight instructor limitations and qualifications.
- Section 61.413, What are the privileges of my flight instructor certificate with a sport pilot rating?
- Section 61.415, What are the limits of a flight instructor certificate with a sport pilot rating?

1-4. FOCUS. This AC is for General Aviation (GA) pilots holding sport or higher grades of pilot certificates who wish to maintain currency and to certificated flight instructors (CFI) who give flight instruction to support such activities.

1-5. RELATED READING MATERIALS. You should discuss the practical test standards (PTS) document(s) appropriate to the certificates and ratings held by the pilot seeking a flight review during or prior to the review. You can find additional information regarding original pilot certification and addition of category, class, and type ratings in AC 61-65, Certification: Pilots and Flight and Ground Instructors, current edition. AC 61-107, Operations of Aircraft at Altitudes

Above 25,000 Feet MSL and/or Mach Numbers (Mmo) Greater than .75, current edition, provides information on operation of high altitude aircraft. Guidance on advanced training criteria that is available in AC 61-89, Pilot Certificates: Aircraft Type Ratings, current addition, may also be appropriate. The Federal Aviation Administration (FAA), commercial sources, and industry associations such as the Aircraft Owners and Pilots Association (AOPA), the General Aviation Manufacturer's Association (GAMA), and the Society of Aviation and Flight Educators (SAFE) make many additional sources of media on pilot currency and qualification available.

1-6. BACKGROUND.

a. Regulatory Review. In 1997, the FAA initiated a major regulatory review and update of 14 CFR parts 61 and 141to ensure that these regulations conformed to the then-current technological and operational environment and to address future pilot certification needs. That was the last major review of those regulations.

(1) The initial phases of the regulatory review addressed regulations requiring priority action by the FAA as a result of National Transportation Safety Board (NTSB) recommendations and other factors. These recommendations addressed requirements such as the flight review required by § 61.56.

(2) That AC provided additional information for pilots and flight instructors to use in accomplishing flight reviews, but did not address specific maneuvers and procedures, which pilots should consider for various categories and classes of aircraft. Many comments cited a need for additional FAA guidance material regarding pilot certification and currency that would enable the GA public to comply with present currency regulations and to tailor currency programs to individual pilot needs. The comments also cited a need for increased uniformity in the conduct of currency programs.

b. Previous Edition of AC 61-98. In 1987, the FAA issued AC 61-98, Scope and Content of the Biennial Flight Review. That AC provided additional information for pilots and flight instructors to use in accomplishing flight reviews, but did not address specific maneuvers and procedures, which should be considered for various categories and classes of aircraft. In addition, the original intention of AC 61-98 was not to cover other currency regulations or transition training requirements for pilots who had already received certification. The material previously contained in AC 61-98 is available in Chapter 2.

c. GA Pilots. As a result of initiatives designed to encourage voluntary compliance with existing regulations and to maintain and further improve the GA safety record with a minimum of new regulations, the FAA has determined that updated advisory guidance is necessary with respect to the currency and qualification needs of GA pilots. The guidance contained in this version of AC 61-98 provides such information and accomplishes the goals of the flight review and other currency requirements.

1-7. PERSONAL CURRENCY PROGRAM.

a. Currency Criteria. Pilots should design a currency program tailored to their individual operating environments and needs. In some cases, pilots may integrate currency criteria with normal operations to reduce the need for separate currency flights. For example, pilots could incorporate additional takeoffs and landings or specialized takeoffs and landings (such as short or soft field) into a previously-scheduled flight. In most cases, pilots should consider the need for currency beyond that specified by the 14 CFR.

b. FAA Safety Team (FAASTeam). The FAA highly encourages pilots to participate in the FAASTeam's Pilot Proficiency Program (WINGS), which includes numerous forms of training media such as online programs and recommended topics for pilots to review with CFIs. Additionally the FAASTeam conducts safety seminars which are open to the public.

c. Aviation Publications and Commercially-Developed Materials. Pilots should also explore the wide range of publications and other commercially-developed materials available for use in personal currency programs. To ensure staying up to date in regulatory changes and flying techniques, the FAA also encourages pilots to regularly read aviation periodicals.

d. Sources for Developing a Personal Currency Program. For assistance in developing a personal currency program, pilots may consult a wide variety of sources. These sources include:

- Pilot examiners,
- Pilot schools,
- Individual CFIs,
- FAASTeam Program Managers, and
- FAASTeam representatives.

NOTE: For information on local sources, pilots should contact the FAASTeam Program Manager at the nearest FAA
Flight Standards District Office (FSDO).

CHAPTER 2. RECENT FLIGHT EXPERIENCE

2-1. RECENT GENERAL EXPERIENCE. Section 61.57(a) and
(b) specifies the minimum requirements for recent flight experience,
specifically takeoffs and landings, in each category and class of aircraft in order to act as pilot in command (PIC) of an aircraft carrying
passengers.

   a. Requirements Specified in § 61.57(a) and (b). Pilots should
regard these requirements as minimums that should be modified to
address factors such as overall pilot experience, different operating environments, complexity of the facilities used, and variations in
makes and models of aircraft within specific categories and classes. For
example, a pilot may meet recent flight experience in a given make and
model of aircraft but may have operated only in light or moderate wind
conditions from airports with long runways. The pilot should consider
acquiring additional takeoff and landing experience in stronger wind
conditions or at airports with short runways before acting as PIC of an
aircraft carrying passengers in similar conditions. Under some circumstances, the change in the customary operating environment may be
great enough that the pilot should seek flight instruction or refresher
training before attempting solo operations.

   b. Basic Currency and Recent Flight Experience. There are
many excellent sources of information available to pilots who wish
to enhance currency under a variety of conditions. The FAA recommends that all pilots participate in WINGS, which provides online
courses, seminars, and guided flight training; and take advantage of free
online safety courses such as those offered by the AOPA Air Safety
Foundation.

   c. Night Currency Requirements. Night currency requirements
deserve additional consideration. The night experience of most pilots
represents only a small portion of their total flight experience. The
impact of marginal weather conditions on night operations is so significant that pilots should evaluate their own need for both increased
currency and additional planning when contemplating flights under
unfavorable conditions at night.

d. Obtaining Currency for each Make and Model. Special considerations apply when pilots operate aircraft makes and models they do not customarily fly. Analysis of accident data has shown that accident rates increase for pilots with little or no time-in-type in the aircraft flown. Section 61.31(e) specifies additional experience requirements for operating high performance aircraft. For non-high performance small aircraft, basic currency requirements of § 61.57(a) and (b) apply only to category and class. For example, a pilot who meets the requirement in a Cessna 152 would also meet the requirement in a Cessna 172. However, the FAA recommends that pilots attain currency in each separate make and model before conducting passenger-carrying operations. This currency should include familiarity with the pilot's operating handbook (POH), the Aircraft Flight Manual (AFM), and/or any other available information on that aircraft. The FAA recommends that all pilots obtain a comprehensive checkout in each make and model aircraft from an appropriately-rated CFI. Airmen are encouraged to search for aircraft 'clubs' for information and familiarization on specific makes and models.

> **NOTE: Considerations regarding basic currency apply not only to single-engine land airplanes but to other categories and classes of aircraft, including multiengine aircraft, seaplanes, gliders, helicopters, gyroplanes, and free balloons.**

2-2. RECENT INSTRUMENT FLIGHT RULES (IFR) EXPERIENCE. In accordance with § 61.57, pilots may complete the six required approaches and holding procedures, intercepting and tracking (all aircraft except gliders) in a ground trainer, level 3-or-below flight training device (FTD), or Aviation Training Device (ATD) that meets the requirements of § 61.4 (refer to the current edition of AC 61-136, FAA Approval of Basic Aviation Devices (BATD) and Advanced Aviation Training Devices (AATD)).

> **NOTE: In order to receive flight training credit in FTDs qualified by the National Simulator Program Manager (NSPM) at levels 4 or above, or full flight simulators, such devices must be used pursuant to a curriculum approved under 14 CFR part 121, 135, or 142.**

CHAPTER 3. FLIGHT REVIEW

3-1. STRUCTURE AND INTENT OF THE FLIGHT REVIEW.

With the increasing complexity of the aviation operating environment, CFIs may want more specific guidance on how to structure and plan a flight review and develop contents that are specific to the needs of the pilot under review. The intention of the flight review is to be an industry-managed, FAA-monitored currency program. The CFI must be aware that the flight review is not a test or check ride, but an instructional service designed to assess and enhance a pilot's knowledge and skills.

a. Accomplishing a Flight Review. Under § 61.56(c) no person may act as PIC of an aircraft unless within the preceding 24 calendar-months that person has accomplished a satisfactory flight review in an aircraft for which that pilot is appropriately rated. An appropriately-rated instructor or other designated person must conduct the flight review. The purpose of the flight review is to provide for a regular evaluation of pilot skills and aeronautical knowledge.

b. Completing WINGS (one or more phases). The FAA reminds pilots and CFIs that, under § 61.56(e), a person who has satisfactorily completed one or more phases of the FAA-sponsored WINGS within the preceding 24 calendar-months does not need to accomplish the flight review requirements of this section. AC 61-91, WINGS Pilot Proficiency Program, current edition, describes how CFIs should encourage pilots to participate in WINGS.

c. Completing Proficiency Checks and Ratings. Pilots and CFIs should be aware that, under § 61.56(d), there is no requirement for pilots who have completed certain proficiency checks and ratings within the preceding 24 calendar-months to accomplish a separate flight review. These accomplishments include satisfactory completion of pilot proficiency checks conducted by the FAA, an approved pilot check airman, a Designated Pilot Examiner (DPE), or a U.S. Armed Force for a pilot certificate, rating, or operating privilege. However, the FAA recommends that pilots consider also accomplishing a review under some of the following circumstances. For example, a pilot with an Airplane Single-Engine Land (ASEL) rating may have recently obtained a glider rating, but may still wish to consider obtaining a flight review in a single-engine airplane if the appropriate 24-month period has nearly expired. When approached by pilots seeking advice on such matters, CFIs should consider the factors described in the following paragraphs.

3-2. PRE-REVIEW CONSIDERATIONS. Before undertaking the review, the CFI should interview the pilot to determine the nature of his or her flying and operating requirements. Elements to consider should include, but not be limited to, the following areas:

a. Type of Equipment Flown.

(1) Section 61.56(c)(1) states that to act as a PIC, a pilot must accomplish a flight review in an aircraft for which that pilot is rated. A pilot might hold multiple ratings. In such case, the pilot may take a flight review in any one of the aircraft for which he or she holds a rating or operating privilege and they will have met the regulatory requirement for all aircraft for which they hold a certificate and or rating. For example, a pilot who holds a private pilot certificate with an ASEL rating and a commercial balloon certificate may take a flight review in either aircraft and will have met the requirements of the rule for both. However, a pilot may not take a flight review in an aircraft for which he or she does not hold a rating or operating privilege. For example, that same ASEL rated pilot may not take a flight review in a Multiengine Land (MEL) airplane if he or she does not hold an MEL airplane rating. A pilot who holds only a sport pilot certificate may only take a flight review in a light sport aircraft for which he or she holds an operational privilege. For example, a sport pilot who holds airplane privileges could not take the flight review in a Cessna 172 since that airplane is not a light sport airplane and he or she does not hold operating privileges for that airplane.

(2) The reviewed maneuvers and procedures will vary depending on the category, class, and make and model of the aircraft used. For example, a review in a light multiengine aircraft will be different from one conducted in a small, two-seat tailwheel aircraft that utilizes limited instrumentation. The CFI may wish to recommend that the pilot complete the review in the aircraft most commonly flown, or in a more complex make and model used if he or she regularly flies several aircraft. The CFI may also wish to recommend that the pilot take a review in more than one category/class of aircraft under certain circumstances. For example, a pilot with ASEL and glider ratings may have flown only gliders in the last 2 years but is also contemplating flying single-engine airplanes in the near future. If a CFI is approached by a pilot who requests a review only in the glider, the CFI may wish to recommend an additional review by a qualified person in a single-engine airplane before the pilot acts as PIC of a single-engine airplane.

b. Nature of Flight Operations. The CFI should consider the type of flying usually done by the pilot before establishing the review plan for conducting his or her review. For example, a pilot conducting long-distance flights between busy terminal areas may need a different review than a pilot who usually flies in the local area from the same airport. The CFI should consider the need for an in-depth review of certain subjects or procedures if the type of flight operations is likely to change, or if other extenuating circumstances exist. For example, a pilot who normally conducts only local flight operations may plan to begin flying to a location with Class B airspace. Another pilot may only operate a two-seat aircraft without radio but will operate in close proximity to Class B airspace. In both cases, the CFI should include Class B airspace operating requirements and procedures in the flight review. This review should also include pertinent revisions to operational regulations to ensure that the pilot has full knowledge of these changes.

c. Amount and Recency of Flight Experience. The CFI should review the pilot's logbook to determine total flight time, time-in-type, and recency of experience in order to evaluate the need for particular maneuvers and procedures in the review. For example, a pilot who has not flown in several years may require an extensive review of basic maneuvers from the PTS appropriate to that pilot's certificate level. Pilots should pay particular attention to the special-emphasis areas found in the PTS. The same pilot may also require a more extensive review of 14 CFR part 91, including changes in airspace and other requirements. Another pilot who is upgrading to a newer or faster airplane should receive more emphasis on knowledge of aircraft systems and performance, or in cross-country procedures appropriate to a faster airplane. Regardless of flight experience, the CFI should ensure that the review plan includes all areas in which he or she determines that the pilot should receive training in order to operate safely. In some cases, the CFI may wish to recommend that the pilot accomplishes a complete refresher program.

d. Agreement on the Conduct of the Review. After completing the above analysis, the CFI should review these considerations with the pilot and reach an understanding regarding how he or she will conduct the review. The CFI may wish to provide the pilot with reading materials or recommend publications for study before actually undertaking the flight review. The CFI should also review the criteria for satisfactory completion of the review with the pilot.

e. Instructor Qualifications. Instructors should also consider their own experience and qualifications in a given make and model aircraft prior to giving a review in that model. The CFI conducting a flight review must hold a category, class, and (if appropriate) type rating on his or her pilot certificate. Also, the instructor must have a category and class rating on his or her flight instructor certificate or a sport instructor privilege in his or her logbook appropriate to the aircraft in which he or she conducts the review. To conduct a flight review in a multiengine airplane, the instructor must hold an airplane multiengine rating on their pilot and flight instructor certificates. For aircraft in which the CFI is not current or with which he or she is not familiar, he or she must obtain recent flight experience or sufficient knowledge of aircraft limitations, characteristics, and performance before conducting the review. In any case, the CFI must observe the rating limitations of § 61.195(b).

3-3. PLANNING AND RECORDING THE REVIEW. The CFI may wish to use FAA's online guidance available at www.faa.gov (see "Conducting an Effective Flight Review") to prepare, conduct, and document the flight review. Some of the material from this optional guide appears in the appendices. After reaching an agreement on how the CFI will conduct the review, he or she should prepare a plan for completing the review. The plan should include a list of regulatory subjects that the CFI will cover, the maneuvers and procedures that the pilot will need to accomplish, the anticipated sequence in which the segments will occur, and the location where the CFI will perform the review. You can find a suggested plan format in Appendix 1. Although not required by § 61.189, the CFI may wish to retain this plan for an appropriate time period as a record of the scope and content of the review.

a. Review of Part 91 Operating and Flight Rules. The CFI should tailor the review of general operating and flight rules to the needs of the pilot under review. The objective is to ensure that the pilot can comply with all regulatory requirements and operate safely in various types of airspace under an appropriate range of weather conditions. As a result, the CFI should conduct a review that is broad enough to meet this objective, yet provide a more comprehensive review in those areas in which the pilot's knowledge is weaker. In the latter instance, the CFI may wish to employ a variety of references/sources, such as the Aeronautical Information Manual (AIM), to ensure that the pilot's knowledge meets current standards.

b. Pilot Deviations (PD). The occurrence of incidents and PDs has emphasized the need to ensure that all pilots receive adequate briefing on PD avoidance awareness. PDs are broadly categorized as airborne or ground. Airborne PDs include altitude and heading deviations, and airspace violations. Ground PDs include runway incursions and any other unauthorized operation in the movement areas of an airport. Pilots should be familiar with all types of airspace, and ground operating procedures, and best practices to avoid potential PDs. The flight review may be the only regular proficiency and recurrency training experienced by some pilots. Therefore, CFIs should place appropriate emphasis on this part of the review.

c. Review of Maneuvers and Procedures.

(1) The maneuvers and procedures covered during the review are those which, in the opinion of the CFI conducting the review, are necessary for the pilot to perform in order to demonstrate that he or she can safely exercise the privileges of his or her pilot certificate. Accordingly, the CFI should evaluate the pilot's skills and knowledge to the extent necessary to ensure that he or she can safely operate within regulatory requirements throughout a wide range of conditions. The CFI should always include abnormal and emergency procedures applicable to the aircraft flown in the flight review.

(2) The CFI may wish to prepare a preliminary plan for the flight review based on an interview or other assessment of the pilot's qualifications and skills. See Appendix 1 for suggested interview questions. Appendix 5 provides a sample CFI flight review checklist. The CFI should outline a sequence of maneuvers to the pilot taking the review. For example, this may include a cross-country flight to another airport with maneuvers accomplished while en route. It could also include a period of simulated instrument flight time. The CFI should request that the pilot conduct whatever preflight preparation is necessary to complete the planned flight. This preparation should include all items required in part 91, § 91.103, such as checking weather, calculating required runway lengths, calculating Weight and Balance (W&B), completing a flight log, filing a flight plan, and conducting the preflight inspection.

(3) Before beginning the flight portion of the review, the CFI should discuss various operational areas with the pilot. This oral review should include, but not be limited to, areas such as aircraft systems, speeds, performance, meteorological and other hazards (e.g., windshear and wake turbulence), operations in controlled airspace, and abnormal and emergency procedures. The emphasis during this discussion should be on practical knowledge of recommended procedures and regulatory requirements.

(4) Regardless of the pilot's experience, the CFI may wish to review at least those maneuvers considered critical to safe flight, such as stalls, slow flight, and takeoffs and landings. Based on his or her in-flight assessment of the pilot's skills, the CFI may wish to add other maneuvers from the PTS appropriate to the pilot's grade of certificate. All reviews should include those areas within the PTS identified as "Special Emphasis." Appendix 5 includes a list of suggested maneuvers. The FAA does not intend this list to be all-inclusive, nor does it limit a CFI's discretion in selecting other appropriate maneuvers and procedures. To the greatest possible extent, the CFI should organize and sequence the selected maneuvers in a realistic scenario appropriate to the kind of flying normally done by the pilot.

(5) The role of the CFI during the review is to provide an evaluation. However, the instructor is not limited to this role and may provide specific instruction to an airman on any areas the instructor notes as being weak. This additional instruction does not preclude the pilot's successful completion of the review as long as the deficiencies are corrected. If the additional instruction does not correct the deficiencies, and/or it becomes apparent to the instructor that additional flights will be necessary, the CFI should discuss the situation with the pilot and proceed accordingly.

3-4. POST-REVIEW CONSIDERATIONS. Upon completion of the review, the CFI should complete the summary and evaluation portion of the flight review checklist (if used) and debrief the pilot. Whether or not the review was satisfactory, the CFI should provide the pilot with a comprehensive analysis of his or her performance, including suggestions for improving any weak areas. The current edition of FAA-H-8083-9, Aviation Instructor's Handbook, chapter 5, provides specific suggestions for conducting the postflight evaluation discussion as a "collaborative critique."

a. Unsatisfactory Completion of the Review. The FAA does not intend the flight review to be a check ride. If the review is not satisfactory, the CFI should log the flight as "dual instruction given" and not as a "failure." The CFI should then recommend additional training in the areas of the review that were unsatisfactory. A pilot who does not receive an endorsement for a satisfactory flight review may continue to exercise the privileges of his or her certificate, provided that a period of 24 calendar-months has not elapsed since the pilot's last successful flight review or pilot proficiency check.

b. Satisfactory Completion of the Review. When the applicant has successfully completed the review, the CFI should endorse the pilot's logbook to certify that the pilot has satisfactorily accomplished the flight review. The CFI should make the endorsement for a satisfactory review in accordance with AC 61-65. The flight and ground time must also be logged in the pilot's logbook in accordance with § 61.51(a)(1).

The remainder of this AC has been intentionally left out of this book.

FAA Guidance Document:
*Conducting an Effective Flight Review**

Appendix 3

3 **Appendix**

Acknowledgements

This guide has been developed with assistance, contributions, and suggestions from a number of general aviation pilots and flight instructors. Special thanks are due to Pat Cannon, Turbine Aircraft Services; Jens Hennig, General Aviation Manufacturers Association; Sandy and JoAnn Hill, National Association of Flight Instructors; Sean Lane, ASA Publishing; Jim Lauerman, Avemco; Stan Mackiewicz, National Air Transportation Association; Arlynn McMahon, Aero-Tech Incorporated; Tim McSwain, USAIG; Rusty Sachs, National Association of Flight Instructors; Roger Sharp, Cessna Pilot Centers; Jackie Spanitz, ASA; Howard Stoodley, Manassas Aviation Center; Michele Summers, Embry-Riddle Aeronautical University; and Max Trescott, SJFlight.

It is intended to be a living document that incorporates comments, suggestions, and ideas for best practices from GA instructors like you. Please direct comments and ideas for future iterations to:

susan.parson@faa.gov

Happy — and safe—flying!

Introduction

General aviation (GA) pilots enjoy a level of flexibility and freedom unrivaled by their aeronautical contemporaries. Airline, corporate, and military flight operations are all strictly regulated, and each uses a significant degree of internal oversight to ensure compliance. GA has relatively few of these regulatory encumbrances. As a result, safety depends heavily upon the development and maintenance of each individual pilot's basic skills, systems knowledge, and aeronautical decision-making skills.

The purpose of the flight review required by Title 14 of the Code of Federal Regulations (14 CFR) 61.56 is to provide for a regular evaluation of pilot skills and aeronautical knowledge. AC 61-98A states that the flight review is also intended to offer pilots the opportunity to design a personal currency and proficiency program in consultation with a certificated flight instructor (CFI). In effect, the flight review is the aeronautical equivalent of a regular medical checkup and ongoing health improvement program. Like a physical exam, a flight review may have certain "standard" features (e.g., review of specific regulations and maneuvers). However, just as the physician should tailor the exam and follow-up to the individual's characteristics and needs, the CFI should tailor both the flight review and any follow-up plan for training and proficiency to each pilot's skill, experience, aircraft, and personal flying goals.

To better accomplish these objectives, this guide, intended for use in conjunction with AC 61-98A, offers ideas for conducting an effective flight review. It also provides tools for helping that pilot develop a personalized currency, proficiency, risk management, and "aeronautical health maintenance and improvement" program. A key part of this process is the development of risk management strategies and realistic personal minimums. You can think of these minimums as individual "operations specifications" that can help guide the pilot's decisions and target areas for personal proficiency flying and future training.

Step 1: Preparation

Managing Expectations:
You have probably seen it, or perhaps even experienced it yourself: pilot and CFI check the clock, spend *exactly* one hour reviewing 14 CFR Part 91 operating rules, and then head out for a quick pass through the basic maneuvers generally known as "airwork." The pilot departs with a fresh flight review endorsement and, on the basis of the minimum two hours required in 14 CFR 61.56, can legally operate for the next two years. This kind of flight review may be adequate for some pilots, but for others — especially those who do not fly on a regular basis — it is not. To serve the aviation safety purpose for which it was intended, therefore, the flight review must be far more than an exercise in watching the clock and checking the box.

AC 61-98A states that the flight review is "an instructional service designed to assess a pilot's knowledge and skills." The regulations are even more specific: 14 CFR 61.56 states that the person giving the flight review has the discretion to determine the maneuvers and procedures necessary for the pilot to demonstrate "safe exercise of the privileges of the pilot certificate." It is thus a proficiency-based exercise, and it is up to you, the instructional service provider, to determine how much time and what type of instruction is required to ensure that the pilot has the necessary knowledge and skills for safe operation.

Managing pilot expectations is key to ensuring that you don't later feel pressured to conduct a "minimum time" flight review for someone whose aeronautical skills are rusty. When a pilot schedules a flight review, use the "Pilot's Aeronautical History for Flight Review" form in this Appendix (on Page A3–19) to find out not only about total time, but also about type of flying (e.g., local leisure flying, or cross-country flying for personal transportation) and recent flight experience. You also need to know if the pilot wants to combine the flight review with a new endorsement or aircraft checkout. Offer an initial estimate of how much time to plan for ground and flight training. How much time is "enough" will vary from pilot to pilot. Someone who flies the same airplane 200 hours every year may not need as much time as someone who has logged only 20 hours since the last flight review, or a pilot seeking a new endorsement in conjunction with the flight review. For pilots who have not flown at all for several years, a useful "rule of thumb" is to plan one hour of ground training and one hour of flight training for every year the pilot has been out of the cockpit. As appropriate, you can also suggest time in an aircraft training device (ATD), or a session of night flying for pilots whose activities include flying (especially VFR) after dark.

In preparation for the flight review session, give the pilot two assignments.

Review of Part 91: The regulations (14 CFR 61.56) state that the flight review must include a review of the current general operating and flight rules set out in Part 91. The *Aeronautical Information Manual* (AIM) also contains information that pilots need to know. Have the pilot complete the Flight Review Preparation Course now available in the Aviation Learning Center at **www.faasafety.gov** in advance of your session and bring a copy of the completion certificate to the flight review. The online course lets the pilot review material at his or her own pace and focus attention on areas of particular interest. Alternatively, provide a copy of the "Regulatory Review Guide" (starting on Page A3–20) as a self-study guide.

Cross-Country Flight Plan Assignment:
Many people learn to fly for personal transportation, but the cross-country flight planning skills learned for practical test purposes can become rusty if they are not used on a regular basis. Structuring the flight review as a short cross-country (i.e., 30–50 miles from the home airport) is an excellent way to refresh the pilot's flight planning skills. Ask the pilot to plan a VFR cross-country to another airport, ideally one that he or she has not previously visited. Be sure to specify that the flight plan should include consideration of runway lengths, weather, expected aircraft performance, alternatives, length of runways to be used, traffic delays, fuel requirements, terrain avoidance strategies, and NOTAM/TFR informa-

tion. The *GA Pilot's Guide to Preflight Weather Planning, Weather Self-Briefings, and Weather Decision-Making* may be of help to the pilot in this part of the exercise. Proficiency in weight and balance calculations is critical as well. If the pilot regularly flies with passengers, consider asking for calculations based on maximum gross weight.

It is within your discretion to require a "manual" flight plan created with a sectional chart, plotter, and E6-B. In real-world flying, however, many pilots today use online flight planning software for basic information and calculations. Appropriate use of these tools can enhance safety in several ways: they provide precise course and heading information; the convenience may encourage more consistent use of a flight plan; and automating manual calculations leaves more time to consider weather, performance, terrain, alternatives, and other aspects of the flight. Encouraging the pilot to use his or her preferred online tool will give you a more realistic picture of real-world behavior, and the computer-generated plan will give you an excellent opportunity to point out both the advantages and the potential pitfalls of this method.

Step 2: Ground Review

The regulations (14 CFR 61.56) specify only that the ground portion of the flight review must include "a review of the current general operating and flight rules of Part 91." This section offers guidance on conducting that review. It also provides guidance on additional topics that you should address. These include:

- Review and discussion of the pre-assigned cross-country (XC) flight plan, with special emphasis on weather and weather decision-making; risk management and individual personal minimums; and

- General aviation security (TFRs, aircraft security, and airport security).

Regulatory Review. Since most GA pilots do not read rules on a regular basis, this review is an important way to refresh the pilot's knowledge of information critical to aviation safety, as well as to ensure that he or she stays up-to-date on changes since the last flight review or formal aviation training session. If the pilot has completed the online flight review course in advance, you will want to review the results and focus primarily on those questions the pilot answered incorrectly. If the pilot has done nothing to prepare, the "Regulatory Review Guide" (*see* Page A3–20) is one way to guide your discussion. You might also organize the rules as they relate to the pre-assigned cross-country flight plan that you will discuss. The important thing is to put the rules and operating procedures into a context that is relevant and meaningful to the pilot, as opposed to the sequential approach that encourages rote memorization rather than higher levels of understanding.

XC Flight Plan Review: At the most basic level, you are reviewing the pre-assigned flight plan for accuracy and completeness (i.e., are the

calculations correct? Did the pilot show understanding of the 14 CFR 91.103 requirement to become familiar with "all" available information?) You may want to use the "Pilot's Cross-Country Checklist" as a guide for checking the completeness of the pre-assigned plan.

If the pilot used automated tools to develop the flight plan, here are some questions and issues that you should teach him or her to ask about the computer-generated package:

- How do I know that the computer-generated information is correct? (*Not all online flight planning and flight information tools are the same. Some provide real-time updates; others may be as dangerous as an out-of-date chart.*)

- Does the computer-generated information pass the "common sense" test? (*Garbage-in, garbage-out is a fundamental principle in any kind of automation. If a pilot headed for Augusta, Georgia (KAGS) mistakenly asks for KAUG, the resulting flight plan will go to Augusta, Maine instead.*)

- Does this plan include all the information I am required to consider? (*Some planning tools compute only course and distance, without regard to wind, terrain, performance, and other factors in a safety-focused flight plan*).

- Does this plan keep me out of trouble? (*What if the computer-proposed course takes you through high terrain in high density altitude conditions?*)

- What will I do if I cannot complete the flight according to this plan? (*Weather can always interfere, but pilots should also understand that flight planning software does not always generate ATC-preferred routes for IFR flying.*)

Each of these questions is directed to a critical point that you should emphasize: automated flight planning tools can be enormously helpful, but the pilot must *always* review the information with a critical eye, *frequently* supplement the computer's plan with additional information, and *never* simply assume that the computer-generated package "must be" okay because the machine is smarter.

Asking these kinds of questions is key to critical thinking, which is in turn the secret to good aeronautical decision-making (ADM) and risk management. There are many models for ADM, including charts that provide quantitative assessment and generate a numerical "score" that pilots can use in evaluating the level of risk. Although these tools can be useful, you may want to present the "3–P" method developed by the FAA Aviation Safety Program. This model encourages the pilot to **P**erceive hazards, **P**rocess risk level, and **P**erform risk management by asking a series of questions about various aspects of the flight. The "3–P Risk Management Process" handout in this Appendix (on Page A3–23) explains this method in detail.

Since statistics show that weather is still the factor most likely to result in accidents with fatalities, the XC flight plan assignment also provides an important opportunity to discuss weather and weather decision-making. The *GA Pilot's Guide to Preflight Weather Planning, Weather Self-Briefings, and Weather Decision-Making*, which uses the 3–P method as a framework for weather decision-making, might be helpful in this discussion. If the pilot flies VFR at night, be sure to talk about night flying considerations, especially in overcast or "no moon" conditions.

GA Security: In the post-September 11 security environment, any security incident involving general aviation pilots, aircraft, and airports can prompt calls for new restrictions. As a flight instructor, you have a special responsibility to ensure that your clients know and follow basic security procedures. These include not only respect for temporary flight restrictions (TFRs), but also for the importance of securing your aircraft against unauthorized use. Pilots should never leave the aircraft unlocked or, worse, unattended with the keys inside.

In addition, be sure that the pilot knows about the Airport Watch Program, which was developed by the Transportation Security Administration (TSA) and the Aircraft Owners and Pilots Association (AOPA). Airport Watch relies upon the nation's pilots to observe and report suspicious activity. The Airport Watch Program is supported by a government-provided toll free hotline (1-866-GA-SECURE) and system for reporting and acting on information provided by general aviation pilots. A "General Aviation Security" checklist of what to look for is included in this Appendix (on Page A3–24). For more information on GA security, see TSA's GA security website and AOPA's online GA security resources page.

For specific information on flying in security-restricted airspace, including the Washington DC metropolitan area Air Defense Identification Zone (ADIZ), direct pilots to the FAA's new online ADIZ–TFR training course and to the Air Safety Foundation's online airspace training courses.

Step 3: Flight Activities

To operate safely in the modern flight environment, the pilot needs solid skills in three distinct, but interrelated, areas. These include:

"Physical Airplane" Skills
(i.e., basic stick-and-rudder proficiency);

"Mental Airplane" Skills
(i.e., knowledge and proficiency
in aircraft systems);

Aeronautical Decision-Making (ADM)
Skills (i.e., higher-order thinking skills).

Many flight reviews consist almost exclusively of airwork followed by multiple takeoffs and landings. These maneuvers can give you a very good snapshot of the pilot's "physical airplane" skills. They are also good for the pilot, who gets a safe opportunity to practice proficiency maneuvers that he or she may not have performed since the last flight review. Airwork alone, however, will tell you little about the pilot's "mental airplane" knowledge of avionics and other aircraft systems, and even less about the pilot's ability to make safe and appropriate decisions in real-world flying (ADM). Therefore, you need to structure the exercise to give you a clear picture of the pilot's skills with respect to each area.

Having the pilot fly the cross-country trip you assigned and discussed in the ground review is a good way to achieve this goal. One leg will involve flying from departure to destination, during which you ensure that the pilot encounters scenarios that let you evaluate the pilot's systems knowledge ("mental airplane") and decision-making skills, including risk management. The other leg (which can come first, depending on how you choose to organize the exercise) will focus more on airwork, which allows you to evaluate "physical airplane" skills.

Be sure to include a diversion. Remember the computer-generated flight plan discussed during the ground review portion? While you are en route to the planned destination, give the pilot a scenario that requires an immediate diversion

(e.g., mechanical problem, unexpected weather). Ask the pilot to choose an alternate destination and, using all available and appropriate resources (e.g., chart, basic rules of thumb, "nearest" and "direct to" functions on the GPS) to calculate the approximate course, heading, distance, and time needed to reach the new destination. Proceed to that point and, if at all feasible, do some of the "physical airplane" pattern work at the unexpected alternate.

The diversion exercise has several benefits. First, it generates "teachable moments," which are defined as those times when the learner is most aware of the need for certain information or skills, and therefore most receptive to learning what you want to teach. Diverting to an airport surrounded by high terrain, for example, provides a "teachable moment" on the importance of obstacle awareness and terrain avoidance planning. Second, the diversion exercise quickly and efficiently reveals the pilot's level of skill in each of the three areas:

- *"Physical Airplane" Skills:* Does the pilot maintain control of the aircraft when faced with a major distraction? For a satisfactory flight review, the pilot should be able to perform all maneuvers in accordance with the Practical Test Standards (PTS) for the pilot certificate that he or she holds.

- *"Mental Airplane" Skills:* Does the pilot demonstrate knowledge and proficiency in using avionics, aircraft systems, and "bring-your-own-panel" handheld devices? Since many GA pilots use handheld GPS navigators, you will want to see whether the pilot can safely and appropriately operate the devices that will be used when you are not on board to monitor and serve as the ultimate safety net. Appropriate and proficient use of the autopilot is another "mental airplane" skill to evaluate in this exercise.

- *Aeronautical Decision-Making (ADM) Skills:* Give the pilot multiple opportunities to make decisions. Asking questions about those decisions is an excellent way to get the information you need to evaluate ADM skills, including risk management. For example, ask the pilot to explain why the alternate airport selected for the diversion exercise is a safe and appropriate choice. What are the possible hazards, and what can the pilot do to mitigate them? Be alert to the pilot's information and automation management skills as well. For example, does the pilot perform regular "common sense cross-checks" of what the GPS and/or the autopilot are doing?

For more ideas on generating scenarios that teach risk management, see the four pamphlets available online at:

www.faa.gov/library/manuals/pilot_risk/

Step 4: Postflight Debriefing

Most instructors have experienced the traditional "sage on the stage" model of training, in which the teacher does all the talking and hands out grades with little or no student input. There is a place for this kind of debriefing; however, a collaborative critique is one of the most effective ways to determine that the pilot has not only the physical and mental airplane skills, but also the self-awareness and judgment needed for sound aeronautical decision-making. Here is one way to structure a collaborative post flight critique:

Replay: Rather than starting the post flight briefing with a laundry list of areas for improvement, ask the pilot to verbally *replay* the flight for you. Listen for areas where your perceptions are different, and explore why they don't match. This approach gives the pilot a chance to validate his or her own perceptions, and it gives you critical insight into his or her judgment abilities.

Reconstruct: The reconstruct stage encourages the pilot to learn by identifying the "would'a could'a should'a" elements of the flight—that is, the key things that he or she *would have*, *could have*, or *should have* done differently.

Reflect: Insights come from investing perceptions and experiences with meaning, which in turn requires reflection on these events. For example:

- What was the most important thing you learned today?
- What part of the session was easiest for you? What part was hardest?
- Did anything make you uncomfortable? If so, when did it occur?
- How would you assess your performance and your decisions?
- Did you perform in accordance with the Practical Test Standards?

Redirect: The final step is to help the pilot relate lessons learned in this flight to other experiences, and consider how they might help in future flights. Questions:

- How does this experience relate to previous flights?
- What might you do to mitigate a similar risk in a future flight?
- Which aspects of this experience might apply to future flights, and how?
- What personal minimums should you establish, and what additional proficiency flying and training might be useful?

Step 5: "Aeronautical Health" Maintenance and Improvement.

If the pilot did not perform well enough for you to endorse him or her for satisfactory completion of the flight review, use the PTS as the objective standard to discuss areas needing improvement, as well as areas where the pilot performed well. Offer a practical course of action—ground training, flight training, or both—to help him or her get back up to standards. If possible, offer to schedule the next session before the pilot leaves the airport.

If the pilot's performance on both ground and flight portions was satisfactory, you can complete the flight review simply by endorsing the pilot's logbook. However, offer the pilot an opportunity to develop a personalized aeronautical health maintenance and improvement plan. Such a plan should include consideration of the following elements:

Personal Minimums Checklist: One of the most important concepts to convey in the flight review is that safe pilots understand the difference between what is "legal" in terms of the regulations, and what is "smart" in terms of pilot experience and proficiency. For this reason, assistance in completing a ***Personal Minimums Checklist*** tailored to the pilot's individual circumstances is perhaps the single most important "take-away" item you can offer. Use the "Personal Minimums Development Worksheet" (*see* Page A3–31) to help your client work through some of the questions that should be considered in establishing "hard" personal minimums, as well as in preflight and inflight decision making.

Personal Proficiency Practice Plan: Flying just for fun is one of the most wonderful benefits of being a pilot, but many pilots would appreciate your help in developing a plan for maintaining and improving basic aeronautical skills. You might use the suggested flight profile in this Appendix as a guide for developing a regular practice plan.

Training Plan: Discuss and schedule any additional training the pilot may need to achieve individual flying goals. For example, the pilot's goal might be to develop the competence and confidence needed to fly at night, or to lower personal minimums in one or more areas. Another goal might be completion of another phase in the FAA's Pilot Proficiency (***WINGS***) Program, or obtaining a complex, high performance, or tailwheel endorsement. Use "Personal Aeronautical Goals" form on Page A3–33 to document the pilot's aeronautical goals and develop a specific training plan to help him or her achieve them.

The flight review is vital link in the general aviation safety chain. As a person authorized to conduct this review, you play a critical role in ensuring that it is a meaningful and effective tool for maintaining and enhancing GA safety.

CFI's Flight Review Checklist

Step 1: Preflight Review Actions

☐ Scheduling

☐ Pilot's Aeronautical History

☐ Part 91 Review Assignment

☐ Cross-Country Flight Plan Assignment

Step 2: Ground Discussion

☐ Regulatory Review

☐ Cross-Country Flight Plan Review

☐ Risk Management and Personal Minimums

Step 3: Conducting the Flight

☐ Physical Airplane (basic skills)

☐ Mental Airplane (systems knowledge)

☐ Aeronautical Decision-Making

Step 4: Postflight Discussion

☐ Replay, Reflect, Reconstruct, Redirect

☐ Questions

Step 5: Aeronautical Health Maintenance and Improvement Plan

☐ Personal Minimums Checklist

☐ Personal Proficiency Practice Plan

☐ Training Plan (if desired)

☐ Resources List

Pilot's Aeronautical History for Flight Review

Pilot's Name: _____ CFI: _____

Address: _____

Phone(s): _____ e-mail: _____

Type of Pilot Certificate(s):

Private _____   Commercial _____   ATP _____   Flight Instructor _____

Rating(s):

Instrument _____   Multiengine _____

Experience (Pilot):

Total time _____   Last 6 months _____   Avg hours/month _____

Time logged since last flight review _____   Since last IPC _____

Experience (Aircraft):

Aircraft type(s) you fly _____

_____

Aircraft used most often _____

For this aircraft:

Total time _____   Last 6 months _____   Avg hours/month _____

Experience (Flight environment):

Since your last flight review, approximately how many hours have you logged in:

Day VFR _____   Day IFR _____   IMC _____

Night VFR _____   Night IFR _____

Mountainous terrain _____   Overwater flying _____

Airport with control tower _____ Airport w/o control tower _____

Type of Flying (External factors):

What percentage of your flying is for:

Pleasure _____   Business _____   Local _____   XC _____

Personal Skills Assessment:

What are your strengths as a pilot? _____

What do you most want to practice/improve? _____

What are your aviation goals? _____

Regulatory Review Guide

Pilot	**Experience**
	    Recent flight experience (61.57)
	Responsibility
	    Authority (91.3)
	    ATC Instructions (91.123)
	    Preflight action (91.103)
	    Safety belts (91.107)
	    Flight crew at station (91.105)
	Cautions
	    Careless or reckless operation (91.13)
	    Dropping objects (91.15)
	    Alcohol or drugs (91.17
	    Supplemental oxygen (91.211)
	    Fitness for flight (AIM Chapter 8, Section 1)

Aircraft	**Airworthiness**
	    Basic (91.7)
	    Flight manual, markings, placards (91.9)
	    Certifications required (91.203)
	    Instrument and equipment requirements (91.205)
	        –ELT (91.207)
	        –Position lights (91.209)
	        –Transponder requirements (91.215)
	        –Inoperative instruments and equipment (91.213)
	Maintenance
	    Responsibility (91.403)
	    Maintenance required (91.405)
	    Maintenance records (91.417)
	    Operation after maintenance (91.407)
	Inspections
	    Annual, Airworthiness Directives, 100-Hour (91.409)
	    Altimeter and Pitot Static System (91.411)
	    VOR check (91.171)
	    Transponder (91.413)
	    ELT (91.207)

Regulatory Review Guide *(continued)*

enVironment	**Airports** 　Markings (AIM Chapter 2, Section 3) 　Operations (AIM 4-3; 91.126, 91.125) 　Traffic Patterns (91.126) **Airspace** 　Altimeter Settings (91.121; AIM 7-2) 　Minimum Safe Altitudes (91.119, 91.177) 　Cruising Altitudes (91.159, 91.179; AIM 3-1-5) 　Speed Limits (91.117) 　Right of Way (91.113) 　Formation (91.111) 　Types of Airspace (AIM 3) 　　–Controlled Airspace (AIM 3-2; 91.135, 91.131, 　　　91.130, 91.129) 　　–Class G Airspace (AIM 3-3) 　　–Special Use (AIM 3-4; 91.133, 91.137, 91.141, 　　　91.143, 91.145) 　Emergency Air Traffic Rules (91.139; AIM 5-6) **Air Traffic Control and Procedures** 　Services (AIM 4-1) 　Radio Communications (AIM 4-2 and P/C Glossary) 　Clearances (AIM 4-4) 　Procedures (AIM 5) **Weather** 　Meteorology (AIM 7-1) 　Wake Turbulence (AIM 7-3)
External pressures	Personal Minimums Checklist Risk Management (3–P model) PTS Special Emphasis Items

Pilot's Cross-Country Checklist

Pilot

- ☐ Review Personal Minimums Checklist
    - ☐ Recency (time/practice in last 30 days)
    - ☐ Currency (takeoffs and landings, IFR currency if applicable)
    - ☐ Terrain and airspace (familiarity?)
    - ☐ Health and well-being

Aircraft

- ☐ Overall mechanical condition
- ☐ Avionics and systems
- ☐ Performance calculations
- ☐ Fuel requirements
- ☐ Other equipment

EnVironment

- ☐ Weather
    - ☐ Reports and forecasts
        - ☐ Departure
        - ☐ En route
        - ☐ Destination
    - ☐ Severe weather forecasts?
    - ☐ Weather stability?
    - ☐ Alternate required?
- ☐ Night
    - ☐ Flashlights available
    - ☐ Terrain avoidance plan
- ☐ Airspace
    - ☐ TFRs or other restrictions
    - ☐ COM/NAV equipment requirements
    - ☐ Cruising altitude(s)
- ☐ Terrain
    - ☐ VFR and IFR charts with MSA/MEA altitudes
    - ☐ AOPA/ASF Terrain Avoidance Planning
- ☐ Airports
    - ☐ COM/NAV requirements and frequencies
    - ☐ Runway lengths
    - ☐ Services available

External Pressures

- ☐ Family expectations?
- ☐ Passenger needs / expectations?
- ☐ Weather worries?
- ☐ Prepared for diversion (money, accommodations)?
- ☐ Time pressures (e.g., "must be at work" issues)?

3-P Risk Management Process

Good aeronautical decision-making includes risk management, a process that systematically identifies hazards, assesses the degree of risk, and determines the best course of action. There are many models for risk management, including charts that generate a numerical "score." Although these tools can be useful, numbers-based tools suggest a level of precision that may be misleading.

An alternative method is the Perceive – Process – Perform risk management and aeronautical decision-making model developed by the FAA Aviation Safety Program. There are three basic steps in this model:

PERCEIVE hazards

PROCESS to evaluate level of risk

PERFORM risk management

PERCEIVE: The goal is to identify hazards, which are events, objects, or circumstances that could contribute to an undesired event. You need to consider hazards associated with:

Pilot
Aircraft
en**V**ironment
External Pressures.

PROCESS: Ask questions to determine what can hurt you. In short, why do you have to **CARE** about these hazards?

What are the **C**onsequences?

What are the **A**lternatives available to me?

What is the **R**eality of the situation facing me?

What kind of **E**xternal pressures may affect my thinking?

PERFORM: Change the situation in your favor. Your objective is to make sure the hazard does not hurt *me* or my loved ones, so work to either

Mitigate the risk involved, or

Eliminate the risk involved.

General Aviation Security

The Transportation Security Administration (TSA) has partnered with the Aircraft Owners and Pilots Association (AOPA) to develop a nationwide Airport Watch Program that uses the more than 650,000 pilots as eyes and ears for observing and reporting suspicious activity. This partnership helps general aviation keep our airports secure without needless and expensive security requirements. AOPA Airport Watch is supported by a centralized government provided toll free hotline (1-866-GA-SECURE) and system for reporting and acting on information provided by general aviation pilots. The Airport Watch Program includes warning signs for airports, informational literature, and training videotape to educate pilots and airport employees as to how security of their airports and aircraft can be enhanced.

Here's what to look for:

- Pilots who appear under the control of someone else.
- Anyone trying to access an aircraft through force—without keys, using a crowbar or screwdriver.
- Anyone who seems unfamiliar with aviation procedures trying to check out an airplane.
- Anyone who misuses aviation lingo—or seems too eager to use all the lingo
- People or groups who seem determined to keep to themselves.
- Any members of your airport neighborhood who work to avoid contact with you or other airport tenants.
- Anyone who appears to be just loitering, with no specific reason for being there.
- Any out-of-the-ordinary videotaping of aircraft or hangars.
- Aircraft with unusual or obviously unauthorized modifications.
- Dangerous cargo or loads—explosives, chemicals, openly displayed weapons—being loaded into an airplane.
- Anything that strikes you as wrong—listen to your gut instinct, and then follow through.
- Pay special attention to height, weight, and the individual's clothing or other identifiable traits.

Use common sense. Not all these items indicate terrorist activity.
When in doubt, check it out!
Check with airport staff or call the National Response Center
1-866-GA-SECURE!

Developing Personal Weather Minimums

Note This worksheet was adapted from the
Personal and Weather Risk Assessment Guide (October 2003): **www.faasafety.gov**

Certification, Training, and Experience Summary

Certification	Certificate level (e.g., private, commercial, ATP)	
	Ratings (e.g., instrument, multiengine)	
	Endorsements (e.g., complex, high performance, high altitude)	
Training	Flight review (e.g., certificate, rating, Wings Program)	
	Instrument Proficiency Check	
	Time since checkout in airplane 1	
	Time since checkout in airplane 2	
	Time since checkout in airplane 3	
	Variation in equipment used (e.g., GPS navigators)	
Experience	Total flying time	
	Years flying	
	Hours in previous 12 months	
	Hours in this airplane (or identical model) in last 12 months	
	Landings in last 12 months	
	Night hours in last 12 months	
	Night landings in last 12 months	
	Hours flown in high density altitude in last 12 months	
	Hours flown in mountainous terrain in last 12 months	
	Crosswind landings in last 12 months	
	IFR hours in last 12 months	
	IMC hours (actual conditions) in last 12 months	
	Approaches (actual or simulated) in last 12 months	

Note: Use this part of the worksheet to review your recency and currency before a specific flight.

Suggested Personal Minimums

Weather Condition	VFR Pilot (100–200 hours)	IFR Pilot (300–500 hours)	My Personal Minimums
Ceiling & Visibility			
Ceiling–DAY VFR	3,000 feet	2,000 feet	
Ceiling–NIGHT VFR	5,000 feet	3,000 feet	
Ceiling–IFR APPROACH	n/a	Minimums + 500	
Visibility–DAY VFR	5 miles	3 miles	
Visibility–NIGHT VFR	7 miles	5 miles	
Visibility–IFR APPROACH	n/a	Minimums + 1/2 mile	
Turbulence (Wind)			
Surface Wind Speed	15 knots	15 knots	
Surface Wind Gusts	5 knots	5 knots	
Crosswind Component	7 knots	7 knots	
Mountain Flying	Consult instructor or mentor		
Overwater Flying	Consult instructor or mentor		
Icing Conditions	n/a	Consult instructor or mentor	

PAVE Personal Minimums Development Guide (PILOT Factors)

Pilot's Name: _____ CFI: _____ Date: _____

Example below assumes total time is < 500 hours*; adjust as appropriate for additional experience

		Go	Risk Mitigation Strategy	No-Go
Recency (last 90 days)	>6 TO & LDG	X		
	3–6 TO & LDG	X		
	0–3 TO & LDG		Work with a CFI (especially if total time < 100 hours).	
Time in Type (make & model in last 90 days)	>9	X		
	5–8	X		
	0–4		Work with a CFI (especially if total time < 100 hours).	
IFR App (in last 90 days, if filing IFR)	>3	X		
	<3		Plan practice session in VMC before flying in IMC.	
	0		Work with CFI before filing IFR or flying in IMC.	
IFR Time (in last 90 days, actual or sim)	>3	X		
	<3		Plan practice session in VMC before flying in IMC.	
	0		Work with CFI before filing IFR or flying in IMC.	

*AOPA Air Safety Foundation's Nall Report shows that 32% of all GA accidents and 26% of fatal GA accidents involve pilots with total time under 500 hours.

PAVE Personal Minimums Development Guide (PILOT Factors) *continued*

Physical Condition

		Go	Risk Mitigation Strategy	No-Go
Sleep (last 24 hours)	>6 hours	X		
	5–6 hours		Fly earlier in the day; avoid night flying.	
	< 5 hours			X
Food &Water	3 meals	X		
	Missed meals?		Take time for meal (or light snack/water) before flight; otherwise – NO-GO.	
Alcohol (last 8 hours)	0	X		
	Any amount			X
Drugs/Meds	0	X		
	Prescription?		Confirm that prescription meds are acceptable to FAA.	
	Other?		Do not fly if under the influence of any drug.	X
Stress	Any?		Stress from family, work, or other areas can be a dangerous distraction.	X
Illness	Any?		Do not fly if you are sick – even common colds can be distracting.	X

PAVE Personal Minimums Development Guide (AIRCRAFT Factors)

Pilot's Name: _____ CFI: _____ Date: _____

Performance		Go	Risk Mitigation Strategy	No-Go
Fuel Reserves (day VFR)	> 1.5 hours	X		
	1 hour	X		
	< 1 hour			X
Fuel Reserves (night VFR)	> 2 hours	X		
	1.5 – 2 hours		Stay within easy range of airport with fuel available at night.	
	< 1.5 hours			X
Fuel Reserves (day or night IFR)	> 2 hour	X		
	< 2 hours			X
Hours (TO & LDGs in type in last 90 days)	3–6		Work with a CFI (especially if total time < 100 hours).	
	< 3			X
Weight	> MGTOW		If final calculation is close to MGTOW, use precise weights to ensure accuracy.	X
	< MGTOW	X		
CG	In CG range	X		
	Out of CG		Do not operate outside of CG range – redistribute load or do not go!	X
Density Altitude	0–2000	X		
	2000–5000		Carefully calculate performance numbers: TO & LDG, Climb, Cruise.	
	> 5000		Carefully calculate performance; if unaccustomed to high DA ops, do not go!	X
TO & LDG Margins (relative to POH numbers)	> 1000+	X		
	500–1000+		Carefully calculate performance with special attention to chart notes.	
	< 500+			X
Equipment	Avionics		Proficient in operation of all systems?	
	Comm/Nav			
	Charts		Lack of current & appropriate charts is a no-go item!	
	Clothing		Suitable for preflight and enroute conditions.	
	Survival gear		Must have if flying over water, snow, mountains, etc.	

PAVE Personal Minimums Development Guide (ENVIRONMENT Factors)

Pilot's Name: _____ CFI: _____ Date: _____

Airport Conditions (departure & destination)

		Go	Risk Mitigation Strategy	No-Go
X-Wind (assumes max demonstrated XW of 15 knots)	<5	X		
	5–10		Are you current and proficient in crosswind landings?	
	>10		Work with CFI.	
Runway Length (relative to POH numbers)	>1000+	X		
	500–1000+		Carefully calculate performance with special attention to chart notes.	
	<500+			X

Weather Conditions (reports & forecasts)

		Go	Risk Mitigation Strategy	No-Go
Reports (METARS, etc.)	<1 hour old	X		
	1–3 hours old		Be especially cautious if there are changes (e.g., SPECI reports).	
			Get updated weather before departing.	
	>3 hours old		Do not operate on basis of reports more than 3 hours old.	X
Forecasts (TAFs, etc.)	<2 hours old	X		
	2–4 hours old		Be suspicious – especially if TAFs have been amended.	
	4–6 hours old		TAFs are produced for 00Z, 06Z, 12Z, and 18Z. Don't use a "stale" forecast!	X
Icing	Any		Unless you are qualified and your aircraft is certified for flight into known icing, do not attempt to operate light aircraft in forecast icing conditions.	X
T- Storms	Any		Unless you are qualified and your aircraft has thunderstorm avoidance equipment (radar, stormscope, datalink), do not enter clouds when thunderstorms are forecast. If VFR, do not operate unless you can maintain at least 20 nm away from cumulonimbus.	X

Weather Conditions (ceiling & visibility for day VFR)

		Go	Risk Mitigation Strategy	No-Go
Ceiling	>3000	X		
	1000–3000		Ensure that you are current, proficient, and familiar with surrounding terrain.	
	<1000		Not legal for VFR.	X
Visibility	>5	X		
	5		Ensure that you are current, proficient, and familiar with surrounding terrain.	
	<5		Although legal for VFR, visibility lower than 5 miles creates a higher risk.	X

PAVE Personal Minimums Development Guide (ENVIRONMENT Factors) *continued*

Weather Conditions (ceiling & visibility for night VFR)

		Go	Risk Mitigation Strategy	No-Go
Ceiling	> 3000	X	Terrain considerations are a major factor in the go/no-go decision.	
	1000–3000			
	< 1000		Not legal for VFR.	
Visibility	> 5	X		
	5		Visibility below 5 miles creates a higher risk, especially at night	X
	< 5			X
Light	Full moon	X		
	> 1/4 moon	X		
	No moon or overcast		Fly IFR or do not go— a large majority of fatal night accidents occur when there is an overcast or no moon.	X

Weather Conditions (ceiling & visibility for IFR)

		Go	Risk Mitigation Strategy	No-Go
Ceiling (relative to IAP minimums)	> 1000	X		
	500–1000	X	Consider not attempting in single pilot IMC operations.	
	minimums		Unless you are current and proficient in IFR procedures and IMC conditions, do not attempt an instrument departure or approach to minimums.	X
Visibility (relative to IAP minimums)	> 2 miles	X		
	1–2 miles+	X		
	< 1 mile		Unless you are current and proficient in IFR procedures and IMC conditions, do not attempt an instrument departure or approach with less than 1 mile visibility.	

Factors to Consider in Number of Instrument Approach Attempts

Approach Attempts (at same airport)		Go	Risk Mitigation Strategy	No-Go
	Total IFR time		Regardless of total time, do not attempt more than 2 approaches.	
	IFR experience in last 90 days		Regardless of recent experience, do not attempt more than 2 approaches.	

PAVE Personal Minimums Development Guide (EXTERNAL PRESSURES)

Pilot's Name: _____   CFI: _____   Date: _____

Trip Planning Considerations

		Go	Risk Mitigation Strategy	No-Go
Tolerance for Delay	> 2 day	X		
	1–2 days	X	Be ready for changes in weather that might require a change in your plans	
	0			X
Available Alternatives for	Passengers		Do not fly if you are under pressure to meet someone else's schedule, unless you have alternative arrangements in place to mitigate the risk.	
	Waiting family			
	Accommodations			
	Alternative transport			
Equipment	Credit cards			
	Money			
	Prescription meds			
	Clothing			

Personal Trip Planning Matrix

PURPOSE of TRIP		Self	Passenger(s)	Family/Friends/Colleagues at Destination	Risk Mitigation Strategies
Tolerance for Delay	> 2 day				
	1–2 days				
	0				
Available Alternatives	Accommodations				
	Transport				
	Meals				
	Other?				
Equipment	Money				
	Credit cards				
	Prescription meds				
	Appropriate clothing				

Personal Proficiency Practice Plan

Pilot's Name: _____ CFI: _____

Date: _____ Review Date: _____

VFR Flight Profile—Every 4 to 6 Weeks

Preflight (include 3–P Risk Management Process)

Normal taxi, takeoff, departure to practice area.

CHAPS (before each maneuver):

> **C**lear the area
>
> **H**eading established and noted
>
> **A**ltitude established (at least 3,000 AGL)
>
> **P**osition near a suitable emergency landing area
>
> **S**et power and aircraft configuration

Steep turns (both directions), maintaining altitude within 100 feet and airspeed within 10 knots.

Power-off stalls (approach to landing) and recovery.

Power-on stalls (takeoff/departure) and recovery.

Ground reference maneuvers.

Pattern practice:

> Normal landing (full flaps)
>
> Short-field takeoff and landing over a 50-foot obstacle
>
> Soft-field takeoff and landing

Secure the aircraft.

Review your performance.

Schedule next proficiency flight.

Personal Aeronautical Goals

Pilot's Name: _____ CFI: _____

Date: _____ Review Date: _____

Training Goals

_____ Certificate Level (Private, Commercial, ATP)

_____ Ratings (Instrument, AMEL, ASES, AMES, etc.)

_____ Endorsements (high performance, complex, tailwheel, high altitude)

_____ Phase in Pilot Proficiency (*WINGS*) Program

_____ Instructor Qualifications (CFI, CFI-I, MEI, AGI, IGI)

Other: _____

_____

Proficiency Goals

_____ Lower personal minimums to:

        _____ Ceiling

        _____ Visibility

        _____ Winds

        _____ Precision Approach Minimums

        _____ Non-Precision Approach Minimums

_____ Fly at least:

        _____ Times per month

        _____ Hours per month

        _____ Hours per year

        _____ XC flights per year

        _____ Night hours per month

_____ Make a XC trip to: _____

Other: _____

_____

Aeronautical Training Plan

_____

_____

_____

_____

_____

3 Appendix

Advisory
Circular:
AC 61-91J Appendix 4

Advisory Circular

Subject: **WINGS—Pilot Proficiency Program**

Date: 2/16/11

Initiated by: AFS-800

AC No: **61-91J**

1. **PURPOSE.** The objective of the WINGS—Pilot Proficiency Program is to reduce the number of accidents in General Aviation (GA) by assisting airmen to find educational opportunities designed to help them apply the principles of risk assessment and risk management (RM). When properly applied, these principles will help mitigate accident causal factors associated with common pilot errors, lack of proficiency, and faulty knowledge. The Federal Aviation Administration's (FAA) purpose is to encourage the majority of GA pilots, through WINGS, to engage in ongoing, targeted flying tasks and learning activities keyed to identified risks and which are designed to mitigate those risks. The FAA continually collects and assesses its databases to identify the risks associated with GA flying and incorporates risk mitigation strategies into initial and ongoing pilot education.

2. **CANCELLATION.** This advisory circular (AC) cancels AC 61-91H, Pilot Proficiency Award Program, dated April 26, 1996. The FAA accepted applications for awards under the discontinued program through January 31, 2008.

3. **BACKGROUND.** To address accident causal factors associated with common pilot errors, lack of proficiency, and faulty knowledge, the FAA developed a voluntary pilot education and proficiency program (i.e., WINGS) and made it available via the Internet to all pilots at all certificate levels. The WINGS Program consists of learning activities and tasks selected to address the documented causal factors of aircraft accidents. Accomplishment of a phase of WINGS requires the participating pilot to demonstrate proficiency in specified knowledge and skill tasks. The FAA encourages pilots to participate in ongoing aviation educational learning and skill-building events with an instructor. The WINGS Program provides the opportunity, the structure, and the recognition for pilots to continue their aviation education. This ongoing effort fosters new learning, review, and flight proficiency in the areas of operation found in current practical test standards (PTS). The

FAA further encourages pilots to maintain proficiency by using the WINGS Program. To this end, the WINGS Program has three levels of participation: Basic WINGS, Advanced WINGS, and Master WINGS. Within each level, a pilot may earn phases of WINGS as explained below and at www.FAASafety.gov.

4. **DISCUSSION.** Accident data point to specific areas of pilot operations where knowledge, skill, or decisionmaking ability are causal factors in the accidents or incidents. Aviation experts have identified hazards associated with GA flying. Accident and incident data indicate the most common situations where hazards become risks. The WINGS Program targets flying situations and knowledge areas where unmitigated risk is most likely to result in an accident. Prior to the implementation of this new WINGS Program, a review of all aircraft accidents in the United States over a 2-year period was conducted. This review resulted in a list of accident causal factors, by aircraft category and class, which appeared most often in accident reports. The activities and tasks required for completion of a phase of WINGS address these causal factors. For example, poor aeronautical decisionmaking was cited by accident investigators as a primary accident causal factor in many accidents. Hence, the WINGS Program requires successful completion of an activity on the subject of aeronautical decisionmaking as one of the requirements for a phase of WINGS. Likewise, other accident causal factors cited in reports, such as performance and limitations, preflight planning, positive aircraft control, basic flying skills, and takeoffs and landings are required for completion of a phase of WINGS. For the purposes of the WINGS Program, these accident causal factors are conveniently arranged in three knowledge and flight areas as described on www.FAASafety.gov. Required WINGS activities may be revised over time and reflected on www.FAASafety.gov whenever statistical data indicates a change is necessary.

5. **APPLICABILITY.**

   a. **Who May Participate.** All pilots (including student pilots) holding an FAA-issued pilot certificate and any required medical certificate may participate in the WINGS Program. Pilots should request certificated or authorized flight instructors, flight schools, and qualified FAA Safety Team (FAASTeam) industry members to participate with them in the WINGS Program. We encourage FAA-approved Title 14 of the Code of Federal Regulations

(14 CFR) part 142 training centers to invite their customers to participate in WINGS by following the special simulator-based syllabus available at www.FAASafety.gov. Pilots operating under 14 CFR parts 91 subpart K (part 91K), 121, 125, and 135 may also participate and benefit from the safety-related information associated with the WINGS Program. There is no limitation on participation in the WINGS Program for airmen who may have been involved in an accident or incident, as such airmen are encouraged to participate.

b. **Incentive Awards.** Airmen who participate in the program and satisfactorily complete a current phase of WINGS will not have to complete the flight review requirements of 14 CFR part 61, § 61.56. Section 61.56(e) states that participating airmen do not need to accomplish the flight review requirements of part 61 if, since the beginning of the 24th calendar-month before the month in which that pilot acts as pilot-in-command (PIC), he or she has satisfactorily accomplished one or more phases of an FAA-sponsored pilot proficiency award program. Each time a pilot earns a new phase of WINGS, it satisfies the flight review requirement regardless of how frequently or closely spaced the phase or award.

c. **Training Requirements.** Pilots earn a phase of WINGS by successfully accomplishing a specified number of knowledge and flight tasks. The requirements of these tasks, as found in the current PTS, correspond to leading accident causal factors, as described in paragraph 4 above. Each time the pilot successfully completes the specified set of tasks, he or she earns another phase of WINGS.

(1) Pilots must complete all of the required set of tasks for a phase of WINGS, three knowledge and flight activities, within a 12-month period to count toward that phase of WINGS. When pilots complete the set of tasks for a phase of WINGS, that phase of WINGS is valid for 12 months. Current requirements of the WINGS Program are available at www.FAASafety.gov.

(2) The WINGS Program generally requires pilots to demonstrate proficiency in both knowledge areas and flight maneuvers. Although a demonstration of proficiency is not always possible for knowledge activities such as safety seminars, a demonstration of proficiency is always required

for flight activities and online courses. The appropriate PTS contains proficiency standards, including specific tasks for airplanes, rotorcraft, gliders, lighter-than-air, powered parachutes, and weight-shift control. The PTS also includes light-sport category aircraft of all types. Pilots may earn one phase of WINGS in an airplane, another phase in a helicopter, another phase in a hot air balloon, and so on.

(3) Pilots with multiple aircraft ratings select the category and class of aircraft in which they wish to receive training and demonstrate their flight proficiency. Pilots may demonstrate all proficiency requirements for any phase of the WINGS Program in the same category and class, or may demonstrate those skills in any category and class for which they are rated.

6. GENERAL INFORMATION.

a. Tasks. The WINGS Program has two main components: knowledge tasks and flying tasks. While most required activities are automatically selected for the participating pilot, participants may choose some tasks to suit their individual flying needs from a list of activities, events, and seminars, as explained at www. FAASafety.gov.

b. Completion of Knowledge Portion. Airmen can accomplish the knowledge portion in two ways:

(1) Airmen can choose from a broad selection of online courses and safety programs available at www.FAASafety.gov. Airmen receive automatic WINGS credit for successfully completing a qualifying online course.

(2) Airmen may also accomplish knowledge tasks at FAASTeam-sanctioned safety meetings that conform to established selection criteria. Airmen who sign an attendance roster at the event will receive credit for their attendance when the FAASTeam officially closes the event at www.FAASafety.gov. Note that when airmen sign the attendance roster, they must use the same e-mail address that is or will be used on www.FAASafety.gov.

NOTE: Flight tasks are accomplished and skills are demonstrated to a standard of proficiency with an instructor who is authorized to give such flight instruction.

c. **Accessing Accomplishments and Validations.** The airman's accomplishments and validation record is available at the airman's secure WINGS home page at www.FAASafety.gov. Airmen may allow others, such as an insurance company or aircraft rental agency, to view this secure document as necessary. Airmen can also print verification certificates for paper-based recordkeeping.

   (1) Airmen must accomplish flying tasks with a qualified instructor and that instructor must verify that the airman accomplished the selected tasks to the appropriate standards. Airmen can accomplish documentation of these events online when the instructor, or other identified representative, verifies the accomplished work. The pilot may also use the www.FAASafety.gov system to e-mail a credit validation request to the instructor as explained at www.FAASafety.gov. Flying tasks reflect related PTS tasks. The FAA will update the flying tasks whenever a related part of the PTS changes, or when accident data indicates that a change is needed.

   (2) Airmen who do not have access to a computer and desire to participate in WINGS may go to a WINGS instructor, a FAASTeam representative, a FAASTeam Program Manager (FPM), or any person with a computer who can assist the airman in creating a special www.FAASafety.gov account. Airmen who have completed tasks and do not have access to a computer must have those tasks entered at www.FAASafety.gov by a WINGS instructor, FAASTeam representative, or FPM. A description of this procedure is available at www.FAASafety.gov.

d. **Levels and Phases of WINGS.** There are three levels of WINGS:

   • Basic WINGS.

   • Advanced WINGS.

   • Master WINGS.

   (1) The standards for completion of phases at the Basic level of the WINGS Program are generally based on Private Pilot PTS. (An airman holding a sport or recreational pilot certificate may use those standards at the Basic level.) Likewise, the performance standards at the Advanced level of WINGS are generally based on the commercial pilot

standards. For the Master level, they are generally based on the airline transport pilot (ATP) and commercial pilot with instrument and/or flight instructor standards.

(2) Airmen may earn an unlimited number of phases within each of the three levels of WINGS by completing the required activities for a phase of WINGS. The WINGS Program requires all participants to complete Phase 1 at the Basic WINGS level before airmen can receive credit for additional phases or advance to any of the higher WINGS levels. Primary accident causal factors are the basis for the required tasks for all phases at the Basic WINGS level and form a strong foundation for earning additional phases or advancing to higher levels. To reinforce a pilot's understanding of primary accident factors and to emphasize basic knowledge and flying skills, a pilot must complete a phase of WINGS at the Basic level at least once every 12 months.

(3) The design of the proficiency requirements for the advanced and Master levels of WINGS are for airmen who wish to train and study at a level that demands greater proficiency. Once a pilot completes Phase 1 at the Basic WINGS level, he or she may participate at any level. For the Master level of WINGS, airmen must have completed at least one phase in the Advanced level of WINGS. Each airman's My WINGS page at www.FAASafety.gov will acknowledge and record all the accomplishments of that airman in WINGS, recognizing both the phase(s) earned and the level(s) of WINGS within which the airman achieves them. Each level, accompanied by an increasingly higher phase number within each level, indicates the airman's commitment to ongoing and consistent training. Airmen can print certificates with this indication from www.FAASafety.gov for any phase or level at any time.

(4) In addition, since completion of any phase of WINGS at any level satisfies the requirement for a flight review (as specified in § 61.56(e)), the airman's My WINGS page at www.FAASafety.gov will also acknowledge this. Airmen can print a wallet-sized certificate with flight review information at any time.

e. **Instructor Information.** Instructors are an integral part of the aviation community and, by modeling the best practices, play an important role in reducing the number of GA accidents. Because of this vital role, we strongly encourage instructors to earn a phase of WINGS themselves. However, there is no requirement for instructors to hold a current phase of WINGS to provide WINGS-qualified instruction. Instructors are eligible to renew their flight instructor certificate through participation in WINGS. The holder of a current flight instructor certificate, who serves as a flight instructor in the FAA's WINGS program, may renew his or her certificate in accordance with the following criteria, which is contained in the current edition of FAA Order 8900.1, Flight Standards Information Management System (FSIMS), Volume 5, Chapter 2, Section 11. That certificated flight instructor (CFI) must:

(1) Hold a flight instructor certificate that has not expired,

(2) Hold a current phase of WINGS (at any level) at the time of application,

(3) Have evaluated at least 15 WINGS-accredited flight activities (any level) during which the CFI evaluates at least five different pilots, and make appropriate endorsements in the logbook of each pilot for each activity,

(4) Present a record to an aviation safety inspector (ASI) showing that the CFI has met the requirements of subparagraph 6e(3) above within the preceding 24 calendar-months before the month of application for renewal of his or her flight instructor certificate, and

(5) Present a completed FAA Form 8710-1, Airman Certificate and/or Rating Application Supplemental Information and Instructions, to an authorized person for renewal of his or her flight instructor certificate.

> **NOTE: The FAA prefers that the Integrated Airmen Certification and/or Rating Application (IACRA) be used.**

f. **WINGS Program Modifications.** Modifications to the WINGS Program that are minor in nature will be made and explained at www.FAASafety.gov without further need of revision to this AC.

g. **Frequently-Asked Questions.** Additional information about the WINGS Program and answers to many commonly-asked questions can be found on the "FAQ" page at www.FAASafety.gov. Pilots may also use the "Contact Us" link at the www.FAASafety.gov homepage for more complex questions about the WINGS Program.

h. Authorization for Completing WINGS Tasks. An authorized
instructor can record completed tasks of WINGS not recorded
automatically at www.FAASafety.gov in a logbook or
other proficiency record with an endorsement similar to the
following. This provides verification for later recording at
www.FAASafety.gov by an authorized individual:

*"I certify that (pilot's name), holder of pilot certificate No.
XXXXX, has satisfactorily demonstrated proficiency in the
required tasks as outlined in the WINGS—Pilot Proficiency
Program, activity number XXX on (date)."*

"Instructor Name, Certificate Number, Expiration Date, and Signature"

i. Authorization for Completing WINGS Phases. An FPM or
authorized instructor may endorse the pilot's logbook upon
issuance of a phase of WINGS (as verified by a review of the
airman's WINGS completion certificate) as follows:

*"I certify that (pilot's name), holder of pilot certificate No.
XXXXX, has satisfactorily completed a phase of the WINGS
Pilot Proficiency Program on (date) as outlined in the current
edition of Advisory Circular (AC) 61-91, WINGS pilot
Proficiency Program, which meets the requirements for a flight
review as specified in §61.56(e)."*

"Instructor Name, Certificate Number, Expiration Date, and Signature"

**NOTE: There is no requirement for this final endorsement
but an authorized individual may use it to prove that he or
she completed a flight review.**

/s/ *Raymond Lou Co* for

John M. Allen
Director, Flight Standards Service

Flight Review Checklist

Appendix 5

This is a recommended flight review. Procedures may be added or removed at the issuing flight instructor's discretion, based on the individual candidate's needs, goals, and experience level.

Step 1
Preparation

The following is an example of an instructor checklist of questions to ask the pilot applicant taking the flight review.

Name _____ Telephone _____

Address _____

Certificates, ratings _____

Current now? __ yes __ no. If no, how long since current?_____

What type of flying do you typically do? _____

Last training? _____

How much flying time in last year? _____

Aircraft for test (make and model) _____

N number _____

Areas where training might be needed (weak areas) _____

_____

Goals/objectives for flight review (currency in aircraft, completion of
    WINGS phase, etc.) _____

Location of test (including time and date) _____

Class of airman medical certificate or valid U.S. driver's license
    (if applicable) _____

Aircraft—certificates, logbooks, and equipment _____

Logbook flight time records _____

Fee discussed with payment obligation _____

Part 91 review* _____
*(*Candidate can complete FAA online Flight Review course found at
    www.faasafety.gov, bring the certificate of achievement with them to the flight
    review, and/or complete the written exercise as assigned by the flight instructor.*)

Cross-country flight plan assignment _____

Step 2
Ground Review

- ☐ Regulatory review
- ☐ Cross-country flight plan review
- ☐ Weather briefing review; weather decision-making
- ☐ Risk management and personal minimums
- ☐ General aviation security issues
- ☐ Visual inspection of aircraft: airworthiness (inspect paperwork), weight and balance (CG within limits), airplane performance and limitations

Step 3
Flight Activities

Structure the flight portion as an out-and-back VFR cross-country (XC) with one leg to focus on XC procedures (including diversion and lost procedures) and the other leg to focus on airwork.

- ☐ Airmanship (aeronautical decision-making, systems knowledge, use of checklists, collision avoidance, avoidance of hazardous weather, proper use of airspace, communications and navigation)
- ☐ Takeoff (normal, cross-wind, short-field, soft-field)
- ☐ Steep turns
- ☐ Slow flight
- ☐ Stalls (power on, power off)
- ☐ Flight by reference to instruments (recovery from unusual attitudes, straight and level, turns to headings)
- ☐ Simulated emergency operations (emergency landing, equipment malfunction)
- ☐ Landings (normal, cross-wind, short-field, soft-field, go-arounds, simulated forced/emergency)
- ☐ Postflight procedures (after landing, parking, securing)

Step 4
Postflight Discussion

☐ Review knowledge skills (strengths, weaknesses)

☐ Review flight skills (strengths, weaknesses)

☐ Questions

☐ Discuss aeronautical health maintenance and improvement plan (personal minimums checklist, personal proficiency practice plan, training plan if desired)

☐ Logbook endorsement (if satisfactory completion *only*)